CREATIVE
SELECTION

Ken Kocienda was a software engineer and designer at Apple for over fifteen years. After graduating from Yale, he fixed motorcycles, worked in the editorial library of a newspaper, taught English in Japan and made fine art photographs. Eventually, he discovered the internet, taught himself computer programming and made his way through a succession of dot-com-era start-ups, before landing at Apple in 2001, where he worked on the software teams that created the Safari web browser, iPhone, iPad and Apple Watch. Ken lives in San Jose, California, with his wife.

CREATIVE SELECTION

Inside Apple's

design process

during the

golden age of

Steve Jobs

KEN KOCIENDA

MACMILLAN

First published 2018 by St Martin's Press, New York

First published in the UK 2018 by Macmillan
an imprint of Pan Macmillan
20 New Wharf Road, London N1 9RR
Associated companies throughout the world
www.panmacmillan.com

ISBN 978-1-5290-0471-7

3 5 7 9 8 6 4 2

A CIP catalogue record for this book is available from the British Library.

Printed and bound in India by Gopsons Papers Ltd.

Visit **www.panmacmillan.com** to read more about all our books
and to buy them. You will also find features, author interviews and
news of any author events, and you can sign up for e-newsletters
so that you're always first to hear about our new releases.

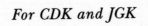

For CDK and JGK

Contents

Contents

CREATIVE
SELECTION

Introduction

This book is about my fifteen years at Apple, my efforts to make great software while I was there, and the stories and observations I want to relate about those times. If you want to know what it was like to give a demo to Steve Jobs, or why the iPhone touchscreen keyboard turned out the way it did, or what made Apple's product culture special, read on.

I'll tell you what it was like to be an Apple software engineer, the pressures and pleasures of working at such a demanding company, and the rush of excitement we coders feel when we make a computer do something new using nothing more than solitude, brain power, and typing.

I'll tell you about the Apple programmer community I became a part of, and how a small group of geeky introverts created a web browser and a touchscreen smartphone operating system starting with only dreams, goals, and ideas.

I'll tell you about how programmers fit into the larger Apple software development system, the joys of collaborating with designers who could bring refinement and elegance to the look and feel of our apps, and the stress of presenting work to colleagues, managers, and executives who always pressed for improvements that seemed just out of reach.

There are many aspects to making products in the Apple way—industrial design, hardware engineering, marketing, legal, and managing a vast international supply chain, to name just a few—but to understand what makes Apple what it is, its *essence*, you need to understand software, and I'll introduce you to the world programmers inhabit, how software gets made from scratch, and how we tried to imbue this software with spirit. While other companies design beautiful hardware, excel at marketing, hire good lawyers, and manufacture gadgets at scale, no other company makes software as intuitive, carefully crafted, or just plain fun. If there's a unique magic in Apple's products, it's in the software, and I'll tell you how we created some of the most important software in the company's history.

When I joined Apple in 2001, desktop and laptop computers were still the company's main products, and while the colorful iMac had been a notable success in reestablishing Apple as a design leader in high technology—Steve Jobs had been back for four years following his eleven-year exile—the company still sat below 5 percent share in a market dominated by Microsoft Windows. Apple certainly had its core enthusiasts at that time, and they were passionate about its products, but to everyone else, the Mac was a computer they might have used in college but forgot about when they became adults and got jobs.

Four months after I started at Apple, things started to change. The release of the iPod was as much a surprise to me as it was to everyone else, and this portable music player kick-started

Apple's shift from computers to personal technology. The iPod also provided the money and the confidence that would lead to the development of the wildly successful devices that followed. This culminated with the iPhone, the product that transformed Apple from a technology bit player into one of the world's most profitable enterprises.

I was a witness and a contributor to these times and these changes. I started programming for the iPhone when the number of software engineers and designers on the secretive project could fit in a small conference room. If you ask me about the first iPad, I might refer to it as K48, the internal code name we developers used before Steve Jobs and the marketing department picked a real product name. Today, on the day I'm writing this introduction, hundreds of millions of people will use these Apple products, and if you count the browsers on Windows and Google Android that use code based on the Safari browser I helped develop, then the number of daily users runs to well over a billion, perhaps it's closer to two.

Yet we never thought about such big numbers. We were too busy focusing on small details. Every day at Apple was like going to school, a design-focused, high-tech, product-creation university, an immersion program where the next exam was always around the corner. With that intensity came an insistence on doing things right, and, without explicitly trying to do so, we developed an approach to work that proved particularly effective for creating great software.

My goal is to share our approach with you—to explain the way we worked. To begin this discussion, I have identified seven elements essential to Apple's software success:

1. Inspiration: Thinking big ideas and imagining what might be possible

2. Collaboration: Working together well with other people and seeking to combine your complementary strengths
3. Craft: Applying skill to achieve high-quality results and always striving to do better
4. Diligence: Doing the necessary grunt work and never resorting to shortcuts or half measures
5. Decisiveness: Making tough choices and refusing to delay or procrastinate
6. Taste: Developing a refined sense of judgment and finding the balance that produces a pleasing and integrated whole
7. Empathy: Trying to see the world from other people's perspectives and creating work that fits into their lives and adapts to their needs

There weren't any company handbooks describing these elements. Nobody outlined this list in a new-employee orientation. There weren't any signs affixed to the walls of our Cupertino campus exhorting us to "Collaborate!" On the contrary, we felt, on an instinctive level, that imposing a fixed methodology might snuff out the innovation we were seeking. Therefore, our approach flowed from the work. This happened from the top down, stemming from the unquestioned authority and uncompromising vision of Steve Jobs, and it happened from the ground up, through the daily efforts of designers and programmers you've never heard of, people like me and my colleagues, some of whom I'll tell you about.

You may have come to this book for a number of reasons, among them to find a from-the-trenches perspective on how an iconic American company worked, to hear the back story on some of your favorite Apple products, or to learn something about the arcane craft of software development. But if you're expecting to read a handbook about the "Seven Elements That Made Apple Great," I hope you'll see that working in the Apple style is not a matter of following a checklist.

While the seven essential elements are a distillation of what we did on an everyday basis, they represent long-term discovery too. An important aspect of this book is the way we built our creative methods as a by-product of the work as we were doing it. As all of us pitched in to make our products, we developed our approach to creating great software. This was an evolution, an outgrowth of our deliberate attention to the task at hand while keeping our end goal in mind. We never waited around for brilliant flashes of insight that might solve problems in one swoop, and we had few actual *Eureka!* moments. Even in the two instances in my Apple career when I did experience a breakthrough—more about these later—there certainly was no nude streaking across the Apple campus like Archimedes supposedly did. Instead, we moved forward, as a group, in stepwise fashion, from problem to design to demo to shipping product, taking each promising concept and trying to come up with ways to make it better. We mixed together our seven essential elements, and we formulated "molecules" out of them, like mixing inspiration and decisiveness to create initial prototypes, or by combining collaboration, craft, and taste to give detailed feedback to a teammate, or when we blended diligence and empathy in our constant effort to make software people could use without pulling their hair out. As we did all this mixing and combining of our seven essential elements, we always added in a personal touch, a little piece of ourselves, an *octessence,* and by putting together our goals and ideas and efforts and elements and molecules and personal touches, we formed our approach, an approach I call *creative selection*.

1

The Demo

"Bzzt." I looked down at my iPhone. I had been nervously turning it over in my hands for the last half hour. Now, finally, I got the text I had been expecting.

It said, "Any minute now."

I replied, "OK."

I had been sitting forward, elbows perched on my knees, fidgeting uncomfortably in an otherwise comfortable leather chair, one of a set arranged as a casual meeting area near the elevators of the second floor of Apple Headquarters, Infinite Loop Building 2, in Cupertino, California. Message received, I got up from my chair, returned my iPhone to my pocket, and walked a few steps down a quiet hallway until I stood outside of the conference room called Diplomacy. When the door opened, I would be invited in to give a demo to Steve Jobs.

It was the late summer of 2009, and I was making software prototypes for a new product, an as-yet-unnamed tablet computer.

A little more than two years before, Apple had introduced the iPhone, which was then beginning to realize its vast potential in the marketplace, just as it had captured the fancy of the computing cognoscenti on the day it was released. Now it fell to people like me, a programmer on the iOS software team, to help create a fitting follow-up.

I'd worked on the iPhone as well, starting in 2005. Through twists and turns, which I'll describe in detail starting in chapter 6, "The Keyboard Derby," it became my job to write the software for the iPhone keyboard, with my main focus on the autocorrect feature, the code responsible for turning your **acxuratw tyoinh** into **accurate typing**.

Throughout the development of the iPhone, we referred to the keyboard, often quite nervously, as a "science project." When we started developing our touchscreen operating system, we didn't know if typing on a small touch-sensitive sheet of glass was technologically feasible or a fool's errand. As commonplace as virtual keyboards have become, in those days, the norm for smartphones was the BlackBerry, with its built-in hardware keyboard, its plastic chiclet keys, and its tactile thumb-typing. In contrast, the iPhone keyboard would offer tiny virtual keys that gave no feedback you could feel with your fingers.

An effective autocorrection feature would be essential, and I worked with the constant worry that my typing fix-up code might turn the iPhone into a punch line. Nobody at Apple wanted a repeat of the Newton, the handheld personal digital assistant the company marketed in the 1990s. Unreliable handwriting recognition gave the Newton a public relations black eye that never faded; the product never sold well, in large part due to its lackluster text entry; and the Newton never became the mass-market indispensable item it was intended to be.

My task was further complicated by Apple's pervasive secrecy. On Purple, the project code name for the in-development iPhone, every detail was protected with need-to-know confidentiality. Few people had been given the chance to see or try the Purple software before Steve announced it in a high-profile keynote presentation in January 2007, so it was out of the question to treat my keyboard work as a real science project and conduct extensive trials on a broad population. I got feedback on the autocorrect feature from just a few dozen people before the whole world got a crack at it. No wonder we were nervous.

Standing in the hallway outside of Diplomacy, I had no time to think about the stress of the iPhone keyboard development cycle. I was focused more on the stress of the moment—an imminent demo to Steve. This new tablet, which Apple would introduce many months later as the iPad, would use the same operating system as the iPhone but would have a larger screen. This brought a new set of keyboard challenges, and I was ready to present my solution for one of them. Demos like this were the foundation of the Apple software development process, as you'll see in the case of this iPad demo and as I'll describe in many other demos throughout this book.

I never demoed my keyboard to Steve while our Purple smartphone was in development—someone higher up in the organization had always done it for me. The success of the iPhone keyboard had, apparently, enhanced my standing. My managers didn't come right out and say so, but their invitation to meet with Steve, coming as it did only after I had proven myself by delivering iPhone autocorrection, showed me what it took to get direct access to the company's famous CEO.

This would be my second Steve demo—the first had happened a few weeks earlier, when I'd shown him font options for the high-resolution Retina display planned for the iPhone 4. That demo had gone well, and since I was being invited back, I began to feel that I had made it into the inner circle of people in Apple product development who would routinely demo software to Steve. I don't know exactly how many people were in this group, but there weren't many. Perhaps a few dozen. Of course, there were even more exclusive circles. I was still in the hallway waiting to be called in, while there were people already sitting with Steve inside Diplomacy.

Steve was at the center of all the circles. When he was in sufficiently good health—he had returned only a couple months earlier from his second health-related leave of absence in five years—he made all the important product decisions. He used these demo reviews as his chief means of deciding how Apple software should look and feel and function.

From my standpoint, as an individual programmer, demoing to Steve was like visiting the Oracle of Delphi. The demo was my question. Steve's response was the answer. While the pronouncements from the Greek Oracle often came in the form of confusing riddles, that wasn't true with Steve. He was always easy to understand. He would either approve a demo, or he would request to see something different next time. Nevertheless, some mystery remained. No matter how good your work was, or how smoothly it had sailed through the preliminary reviews leading up to him, you could never know how he would react. Sometimes he'd say he loved or hated something but then reverse himself in midsentence. Perhaps his change of heart might come a day or two later. Other times his opinions, once stated, held in place for years.

Then there were his moods. On any given day, he might give you a tongue-lashing during a demo if he didn't like the work you brought him. Nobody was exempt either—not top-level executives he worked with every day and not programmers like me whom he didn't know beyond a passing recognition. This was the price of admission to his demo room—either accept it, or don't demo to him. It could be difficult to hang on while riding this emotional workplace roller coaster, and some begged off. One exceptionally talented and experienced colleague told me flat out that he refused to demo his own work in Diplomacy ever again because of the way Steve treated people in these face-to-face meetings. My friend continued to respect Steve's taste, even though he deplored his temperament.

Although Steve's opinions and moods could be hard to anticipate, he was utterly predictable when it came to his passion for products. He wanted Apple products to be great, and he insisted on being involved in the process as it went along, to guide the development of the work through his reviews. That's why I was waiting to show him my demo. He wanted to see my latest progress and then push the work toward his ideal with his feedback and suggestions.

It was a sure thing that our tablet keyboard, a major new user interface element for a new product line, would need his direct approval. Whenever Steve reviewed a demo, he would say, often with highly detailed specificity, what he wanted to happen next. "Add more space between these two elements," or "Replace the green in this graphic with blue," or "None of this is working. Show me more options next time." More generally, he was always trying to ensure the products were as intuitive and straightforward as possible, and he was willing to invest his own time, effort, and influence to see that they were. Through looking at demos, asking for specific changes, then reviewing the changed work again later on and giving a final approval before we could ship, Steve could make a product turn out like he wanted. Much like the Greek Oracle, Steve foretold the future.

I heard a door handle turn. I looked toward Diplomacy, the door now opened just a sliver, and a shard of light from the conference room brightened the darker hallway. As my eyes adjusted, I saw the backlit and smiling face of Henri Lamiraux, vice president of iOS software engineering. Henri cracked the door just wide enough to poke his head out. Even in the moment, I didn't understand this theatrical beckoning. It was common knowledge that Steve saw demos in Diplomacy and that people would quietly come and go from the room on demo day. Yet this was no time to ask questions, and I felt a rush as I headed for the door.

Henri occupied a position where he interacted on a daily basis both with top executives like Steve and with individual programmers like me. He led the team of software engineers responsible for the apps that came as standard on the iPhone—Messages, Mail, Calendar, the Safari web browser—as well as the software kits Apple published for developers out in the world to make apps of their own to post and sell on the iOS App Store. Steve looked to him to deliver on the decisions that came out of these demo sessions, and Henri filled his role with his own brand of self-assurance coupled with a lack of self-importance. He wore a full beard, which he kept cropped close, and over his more than twenty years at Apple it had become less solidly black, more salt and pepper. A Frenchman with a strong accent—occasionally I could understand what he was saying only from the context—he had quaint pronunciations for a number of English words. My favorite was for "build." When Henri said this common programming term, it came out as "bweeld."

Henri had been my manager again for just a few weeks. I say "again" because I had reported to him several years earlier, before the iPhone project, when both of us were in different roles. I'd witnessed Henri's ability to remain calm in stressful situations in an episode when I had sorely tested his patience, and I'll relate that story later.

In the years since, I'd seen him demonstrate his calmness again and again. In the lead-up to a Steve demo, he could be counted on to keep his composure and smile through the tension. Henri acted as a buffer between his team of programmers and the company's hard-to-please leaders. He edited expletives out of the executives' requests before passing them down to individual coders. He might say to me "I just heard Steve reported a bad bug." The actual message he'd received had been more like: "THE F***ING CAPS LOCK BUTTON DOESN'T WORK IN TODAY'S BUILD! DON'T YOU PEOPLE TEST THIS F***ING KEYBOARD?!" As Henri sifted through and related the details at such times, I appreciated his ability to project the confidence that everything would work out. He seemed to know that applying pressure on me wouldn't help me figure out the fix for the bug any faster but that I would drop whatever I was doing and get right on it. In his way, Henri filled a role created by the personality of our intense CEO. He was a source of coolness that prevented us from constantly getting burned by Steve's searing heat.

"Come in," Henri said, smiling as he eased the door open a little more so I could walk through. I took a few steps to cross the hall. Deep breath. The demo was on, or so I thought. Turning to my right as I entered Diplomacy, I saw Steve. He was talking on the phone.

"Yeah, that sounds good," Steve said as he leaned far back in an office chair, staring at the ceiling through round-rimmed eyeglasses, iPhone pressed to his ear, the sleeves of his black mock turtleneck tugged halfway up his forearms, legs crossed in front of him, the cuff of his jeans riding up on his calves to reveal several inches of dark socks above his gray New Balance running shoes. The uniform. He didn't appear to have any lingering ill-ness-related lack of energy, and for the moment, he was directing all his focus toward his phone call. I was surprised for a second or two, but quickly realized that I should stand there quietly and do nothing to draw attention to myself. I was in for more waiting.

It's uncomfortable to listen to someone powerful and mercu-rial as they finish a phone call, and since I didn't want to appear like I was eavesdropping, I put my hands behind my back and surveyed the conference room.

Diplomacy was about thirty feet long and fifteen wide, drab and windowless. A couch in the middle of the room faced the door, roughly dividing the space into two squares. A pair of eight-foot-long tables were pushed against the walls in the half of the room closer to the door. This created an area for demo devices to be laid out, and this was where all the action took place. The couch and tables were arranged end-to-end to form a U, and Steve's office chair was positioned in the crook of the letter, while I stood closer to the open end by the door. I looked down and to my right, onto the table closest to me, and I saw my prototype iPad. It had my demo loaded on it.

Looking around again, I had the same reaction I always did when I set foot inside Diplomacy. The room was shabby, cer-tainly not the decor you would expect in a company as obsessively design-focused as Apple. The table furthest from me only had an iMac on it. On the wall behind the computer, someone had tacked, a bit crookedly, an unframed poster for Mac OS X,* ver-sion 10.2, nicknamed Jaguar. If the poster's tattered appearance

---

*The "X" in this name is a Roman numeral, and Apple says the product is correctly named "Mac O-S Ten." The affinity for obsolete number systems in the naming schemes of the company's flagship products carried over into the iPhone X. Many people pronounce this "X" as "ex," instead of "ten," and who can blame them?

didn't give away its age—it was several years old by then—then its serif "X," rendered with fur and spots, surely did. By that point, this "X" logo had been changed in steps through release after release to metallic gray and then to sans serif. This poster looked seriously dated. As for the tables, they were remarkable for being unremarkable. They weren't the premium examples you might expect, lovingly crafted from the same light-colored wood favored for the display of products in Apple retail stores. No, these were plain, workaday gray tables with Formica tops. Standard-issue office furniture. Floor-to-ceiling whiteboards covered the wall to my left, and they were caked with a heavy accretion of pen marks, indifferently and incompletely erased. And then there was the couch. It was not clean. When you sat down on it, you sank into the cushions as you would on a mangy sofa in a college frat house. In the half of the room behind the couch, there were a couple of forlorn bean bag chairs piled in the corner, an homage to an earlier age in Silicon Valley. On the whole, Diplomacy was a study in indifference. It was an important room, often used for CEO demos, but it was never the center of attention itself.

By now, my glances around the room had killed a minute or two, but Steve showed no signs his call was about to end. I began to feel a self-conscious awkwardness that I was the only one in the room standing, but there was no more room on the couch after Henri sat back down, and Steve was sitting on the only chair. There was nothing for me to do but remain where I was until Steve finished his conversation. At one point, I looked over at Henri, who looked back with raised eyebrows and gave a little shrug, as if to say "I have no idea how long he'll be." I couldn't imagine why Henri invited me in when he did, but again, this was no time to ask questions.

The people sitting with Henri on the couch were the true software development inner circle. They were the few Steve wanted around him to advise, consult, and bounce ideas around as he reviewed demos. They had done this for the iPhone, and now they were there for the iPad too. Each person had earned their place, and kept it, by consistently providing feedback that helped make the products better.

Sitting to Henri's left on the couch was his boss, Scott Forstall, then the senior vice president of iOS software engineering. Scott reported directly to Steve, and he was the one giving me this chance to demo in Diplomacy. Scott expected me to keep it concise and on point when it was my turn to go. He didn't tell me to do that—proper conduct was implicitly communicated through the success and failure of the earlier-stage demo sessions Scott ran himself, where he was the top executive in the room. The stakes in Diplomacy were obviously higher, now that *his* boss was in the room, and since Scott was my sponsor, my demo would reflect on him. Given what I took to be my new probationary status in the Diplomacy inner circle, I imagined that one bad demo might cause Scott to rescind my membership. Even though he never spelled it out, for all I knew, I might be a single bone-headed comment away from never being invited back.

Scott's position was not nearly as precarious. His relationship with Steve was solid, and their partnership extended back to their time at NeXT, the computer company Steve founded after being fired from Apple in 1985. Ever since Apple acquired NeXT in 1996, Steve and Scott had collaborated closely on software.

I expect Steve valued Scott's ability to imagine how new technologies might be integrated into our software products. Scott excelled at making these connections. If a programmer told Scott about an in-the-works software change to the touchscreen system that would make it possible to reliably differentiate between quick swiping gestures and slower panning gestures, Scott could visualize a user feature like swiping on an item in a list, say an email message, to delete it.

The software we created at Apple was an accumulation of such small details. Steve looked to Scott not only to make these kinds of intuitive leaps himself but also to build and lead a team that could make them in volume. This was part of Steve's mission for Apple, the most significant strand of Apple's product development DNA: to meld technology and the liberal arts, to take the latest software and hardware advances, mix them with elements of design and culture, and produce features and products that people found useful and meaningful in their everyday lives. Scott had the position he did because he could make these technology-to-people links as well as anyone, and he could do so with such deceptive ease, sometimes with a complete lack of pauses or throat stroking as he formed a steady stream of on-the-money reactions. His quick-wittedness could be unnerving. I found that Scott could make me feel that I needed to speak faster, so that he wouldn't interrupt to finish my sentences better than I could finish them myself.

Sitting on the other side of Scott was Greg Christie, one of his other senior managers, the day-to-day leader of the Human Interface team, the software designers responsible for the look and feel of iOS and the Mac, as well as the concepts behind how these systems functioned. We shortened his group's name to two letters in conversation, and as the HI team leader, Greg brought breadth and depth to the design of our apps and user interfaces. A flannel shirt–wearing, cigarette-smoking New Yorker, Greg had an encyclopedic knowledge of the history of computing, a tinkerer's knowledge of analog and digital hardware, and a gut feeling for how to create software that made sense to people. A couple years earlier, Greg had given me crucial advice during the development of the iPhone keyboard. At a point when I was desperately stuck, he challenged me, point b.ank, to solve a problem I had been skirting—to make each key smaller than a fingertip and to develop the necessary improvements to my auto-correction code. Greg often provided the insight that some difficult development path was the best way to make our products easier to use. But he was never easygoing. He dragged around a metaphorical bear trap, one that was tripped by lackadaisical effort and bullshit excuses. Try to sneak a slipshod demo past him? You'd get caught in the jaws of a sharp rejoinder, which Greg would likely deliver with a loud snap. He wasn't the most popular man in the company. However, to those who shared his high standards and his abhorrence of lazy justifications, he was unceasingly loyal and supportive.

On the rightmost end of the couch, sitting close enough that Steve could have kicked him with his outstretched leg, was Bas Ording, a designer on the HI team. Bas possessed genius-level skills in illustration, animation, and demo creation, and his deftness contributed much to the intuitive feel of iOS devices. When we needed a way to move up and down a list of items on a touchscreen device that didn't have a mouse or arrow keys, Bas created *inertial scrolling,* the system of finger swiping that speeds up as you scroll repeatedly, glides to a rest when you stop touching the screen, and pleasantly bounces at the end of the list. All of us take this behavior for granted today only because Bas's solution so clearly matched our sense for how this interaction should behave. Tall, thin, with short hair that he spiked so that it stood straight up on his head, Bas had the habit of adding a pleasant "ha-hah" chuckle onto the end of his sentences, as if you and he were in on the same joke together. Bas was one of Steve's favorites. He was one of mine too. I loved working with him. The demo I had for Steve was our latest collaboration.

As I looked again at the faces and postures of these couch-sitters, I noticed that I wasn't the only one trying to appear like I wasn't snooping on Steve as his conversation wore on. The scene started to seem surreal and dreamlike. I looked again at the demo table behind the back of Steve's chair. The iPad was still there—of course it was—but now I wondered: Was the battery charged? Was the dream going to turn into a nightmare?

The work on this keyboard demo had started about a month earlier—soon after I received a promotion to "Principal Engineer, iPhone Software."

My new job was open-ended. I was expected to find, create, and contribute to projects that made our software better. As I tried to figure out what that meant, the HI studio became part of my normal rounds. One day I stopped by to visit Bas. As usual, he was up to something cool.

He'd built a demo using Adobe Director, a software package that, even back then in 2009, was a leftover from a bygone era of computing. Multimedia authors used Director extensively in the 1990s to create content both for distribution on CD-ROMs and for the interactive kiosks you might have found in a shopping mall to help you locate a shoe store or the food court. Flash, the web, and mobile computing had made Director obsolete, but Bas still preferred it, mostly because he was a whiz with the Lingo programming language integrated into the software. This allowed him to create fully interactive demos that superficially looked and behaved like a Mac or an iPhone, even though they were just pictures and animations woven together with a little Lingo code. Even though his demos weren't "real" software we could ship to customers, Director enabled Bas to make quick prototypes that provided a good sense of how the real thing would work.

I looked over Bas's shoulder as he started up his latest Director creation. On the screen of his Mac, I saw what looked like a stretched-out iPhone keyboard. The background, keycap, and key letter colors were the same, but the overall shape of the layout was considerably wider than it was tall. Bas told me this was his proposed design for the iPad keyboard. He'd made this demo to test some variations. Around the edges of his keyboard, Bas had a set of onscreen controls, and as he started to press the buttons and move the sliders, the background, keycap, and key letters on his demo keyboard changed. He made the keycap font bigger and smaller. He switched between light letters on dark keys and dark letters on light keys. He altered the dimensions of the space bar, delete key, and return key, and as they grew or shrank, the other keys changed shape to fill the gaps. Each option was accompanied by a carefully crafted animation that highlighted what was changing. As Bas took me through all his variations, he gave me a quick explanation that made every option seem reasonable and practical. Aside from the beauty of his animations, which succinctly called attention to the detailed differences in his ideas, the aspect ratio and overall key layout made the biggest impressions on me. His proposal for the iPad touchscreen keyboard looked much more like a keyboard on a desktop or laptop computer than the design we had on the iPhone. Punctuation keys and shift keys appeared in their traditional places. There was a number row on top, and these keys displayed the familiar two-character pairings: ! on the same key with 1, @ above the 2, and so on.

A few years earlier, Bas and I had collaborated on the design for the iPhone keyboard, and we'd struggled mightily with the constraints of the phone's small screen size. After many experiments, we'd moved as many keys as possible off the main layout displaying the letters, devoting the reclaimed space to making individual letter keys as big as possible. Even then, a typical finger covered between two and three letter keys. In our final design, we made punctuation and numbers available under a separate layout accessible by tapping a .?123 key. We worried there would be howls and complaints about the inconvenience of this arrangement, but it turned out to be one of those things that people adapted to readily and accepted without much fuss.

As Bas stepped through different options in his iPad keyboard demo, he said he wanted to use the larger iPad screen to revert to a more traditional keyboard layout, like the one for the Mac keyboard on his desk. All along, as we chatted, he continued moving sliders and pushing buttons, and the demo kept up its delightful changes between variations on his general theme of a bigger screen giving us more space for more keys on our new tablet computer. Bas had created a little keyboard playground for himself, and his enthusiasm was infectious. When he finished up his demo and turned around to me, I had a smile on my face.

I returned to my office and thought about the demo Bas had just shown me. I pictured it running on the prototype iPad I had on my desk rather than on his Mac. The clearest image in my mind was the part about adding more keys. That seemed sensible, especially since we had room for more keys on the larger tablet screen. I thought that people would like typing periods and commas without having to tap the **.?123** key.

As I glanced back and forth repeatedly between my prototype iPad screen and the hardware keyboard connected to my Mac, I had an idea. I picked up the iPad, turned it to landscape, and held it up over the Mac keyboard. I noticed that the long side of the iPad screen was about the same width as the top row of letters on the Mac keyboard. It occurred to me that I could take the ten letters from this top keyboard row, **QWERTYUIOP**, and fit them across the width of the iPad screen. There wouldn't be room for number keys above the top row of letters, but that might be all right, since it would result in a design like the iPhone in terms of key layout, but on the larger iPad display, the keys would be almost as big as those on a Mac laptop. This was in contrast to Bas's approach, which was to scale down the full Mac keyboard layout to the size of the iPad display.

Now I had two interesting ideas. My concept would offer bigger keys that would be easier to tap, but users would have to hunt around for numbers and punctuation. Bas's design with more keys would make numbers and punctuation easier to find, but each key would be smaller so they all fit on the display. I decided to make a demo so I could try out both.

I had been responsible for the day-to-day maintenance of the keyboard code until just a few weeks earlier, when I got promoted, so I still knew the software like the back of my hand. I could write the code for two new keyboards in a couple days. I'd add one for the Bas layout with more keys and one for my layout with bigger keys. Building the demo in this way conferred a huge benefit. Unlike the Director demo Bas had shown me, which was just pictures and animations, my demo would be a fully functioning keyboard that would work in any iOS app.

As I thought about it more, I decided to make the keys on my bigger-keys layout match the dimensions on my Mac keyboard as closely as I could. Perhaps I could match the staggered positioning of the key rows as well. If I could mimic this overall geometry, maybe it would make typing on the iPad keyboard seem comfortable and familiar to Mac users.

To make this design work as accurate as possible, I had to take some measurements. I needed a ruler. I didn't think I had one, but I rummaged through my desk drawers anyway, turning up a couple of old RAM chips, a few thumbtacks, and a collection of prototype iPhones, but no ruler. I asked some teammates on my hallway, but I got quizzical looks and shrugs—what does a programmer need to measure? I checked the hallway office supply cabinet. It contained a seemingly endless variety of paper clips, but still no ruler. Then I remembered there was a Target on Stevens Creek Boulevard in Cupertino, about a mile away.

On the drive over to Target, I conjured up an image of the ruler I would get. It would be beautiful, sturdy, made of metal, suitable for a professional draftsman, the kind of precision measuring instrument Apple might make. Target didn't have anything like the Platonic ideal ruler of my imagination. The only ruler it had was one foot long and made of pale blue plastic with yellowish green accents. It looked cheap, and it was. I supposed that the decades-earlier, first-grader version of me probably would have been pleased enough with it, so long as a couple of Iron Man pencils found their way into the shopping cart as well, but honestly, the decisive moment for the ruler came when I noticed I could buy a semicircular plastic protractor in matching colors. Done.

When I got back to my office at Apple with my two new toys . . . *ahem,* tools . . . I started making measurements of my desktop keyboard and its keys, my laptop keyboard and its keys, my iPhone screen and its keys, and the iPad screen. I wanted to create my own personal database of these keyboard elements, to spend time with them, to build a feeling for these objects and their relationships to each other. I jotted down the sizes and angles of everything. I made some sketches in Adobe Illustrator, I overlaid sketches of this on top of sketches of that, and I thought about what to do. I started writing the code I would need to bring two new keyboards online. For the Bas/more-keys design, I would exactly copy the keys on my laptop keyboard, except I would leave off the function key row at the top. For my bigger-keys design, I would model it on the iPhone keyboard in terms of the available keys, but I moved the delete key and added a second shift key. I hammered out some more details, and I spent a couple days writing the code for the demo. Given that iOS already had the globe key to switch between keyboard languages, I treated my two new keyboards as if they were two new "languages." My demo was ready. I went to show Bas.

He responded with a good-natured chuckle, which meant he liked it. He also had a suggestion. He didn't like tapping the globe key to change between these two new layouts. After all, we weren't changing languages. He said that we should add a new keyboard-switching zoom key next to the space bar. Press it once to zoom in to see bigger keys. Press it again to zoom out to see more keys. Bas said he would design an animation for the zooming. I thought this sounded great. I went back to my desk to add a zoom key.

A few days later, we had everything together. It was time to show more people. We put this demo on the schedule for the next round of iPad reviews, where Henri, Greg, and Scott looked at the latest demos. As they reviewed work, they decided whether a design might pass muster with Steve while also estimating

The "more keys" layout Bas designed.

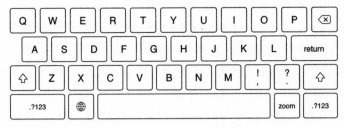

The "bigger keys" layout I designed.

whether Henri's programming team could implement the idea in a high-performance, bug-free manner given the remaining time in the schedule. They were always wary of showing Steve something he might like but that we might not be able to ship in a product. Scott didn't run an ivory tower research and development department. Our demos to Steve carried the promise that we could deliver, and since showing work to Steve implied this willingness to commit, very few demos shown for the first time in these earlier meetings proceeded to him without further refinement. Sometimes there were several rounds of feedback and changes over many weeks before Scott would give the approval to bring the work into Diplomacy.

Our iPad keyboard demo was unusual. We breezed through our pre-Steve review, largely as a result of Bas's ability to tell the story of the software through the zoom animation he'd designed.

When you tapped the zoom button on our iPad demo, the keyboard you were looking at (say, mine) transitioned to the other one (his), much like clicking to go to the next slide in presentation software like Keynote or PowerPoint. The image of one keyboard disappeared to nothingness to reveal the other underneath. Bas added scaling to his animation—the keys of the departing keyboard changed size to match the one coming into view. He also tuned the timing of the animation, so it started slowly and sped up as it went, making you feel you had definitively landed once the animation finished. These effects were subtle, given that his animation was a mere fraction of a second, but Bas had a way of making these details count. When you looked at this zoom key animation, it appeared as if the keyboards were undergoing a complex morph. They weren't. From an engineering perspective, this was significant, since the simplicity of the design meant I could write the code for his animation in just a couple hours. The magic was in the overall effect. The animation didn't look like clicking from one slide to another in a presentation deck. When you tapped on the zoom button, it made you feel like *one keyboard was becoming the other.* The effect registered viscerally. It was exactly the kind of self-explanatory touch that made Apple software easy to use.

Everyone in the pre-Steve review had liked this notion of keyboard switching. We figured users would benefit from more flexibility when it came to typing on this new product. We thought this was an excellent use of the larger screen real estate we had on the iPad as compared to the iPhone. Some people might like a layout with more keys, since they had an intuitive feel for where all the letters, numbers, and punctuation keys were located. Others might like the layout with bigger keys, since they had a tactile sense for where the keys were located under their fingers. It was the best of both worlds. The zoom key made it easy and

pleasant to try both of these two new keyboards and switch between them—there was no need to dig through some preference
setting elsewhere in the system—and Bas's animation made the
feature seem special. Scott gave his approval to show the demo
to Steve.

"Hey, all that sounds good," Steve said, his voice breaking the
near silence in Diplomacy, before saying "Right, I'll call you." His
tone suggested the conversation was about to end, and the rest of
us snapped to back to reality.

Steve said, "Bye," took the iPhone away from his ear, and
focused for a moment on tapping the red button to hang up.
With that, he slid his iPhone back into the front pocket of his
jeans, straightened himself in his chair, and then turned slowly
to face me.

His eyes met mine. Over the years, many people have com-
mented on Steve's special ability to tell you something, whatever
it was, no matter how implausible, and make you believe it. This
reality distortion field, the RDF, has become legendary. Yet, in the
moment Steve fixed his eyes on me, I felt an opposite force, the
RDF with the polarity reversed. Like flipping on a light switch,
Steve had turned on a no-nonsense zone around himself, one
that banished all flummery and neutralized all pretense. His
look wasn't obviously unfriendly or threatening, but surely he
knew his unblinking gaze could intimidate people in my position, and it certainly had that effect on me. I saw his look as a
signal that he wasn't going to let me pull the wool over his eyes.
He was now ready to see my demo.

Scott stood up and crossed behind Steve's chair. "OK, let's
look at this demo. Steve, this is Ken. He worked on the iPhone
keyboard. He has some tablet keyboard designs to show you."
Scott introduced me as if it were the first time I had ever met
Steve, even though I had demoed for him just a couple weeks

earlier. If Steve had fond feelings for my previous work or recognized me from that previous demo, he didn't show a flicker of either. Scott reached out to the prototype iPad without picking it up from the table, he clicked the home button, and when the screen woke up, he slid his finger to unlock it.

Steve was still looking at me. Continuing the demo introduction from where Scott left off, I said, "Right, there are two designs. One has more keys, like a laptop keyboard, and the other has bigger keys, like a scaled-up iPhone. We're thinking of offering both. Try the zoom key to switch between them."

Steve then slowly swiveled his chair around to the demo table. He looked down. In front of him, the iPad was in landscape, with the home button to the right of the display. An early prototype version of the iPad Notes app was running. The insertion point was blinking in a blank document. At the bottom of the screen, the Bas-designed more-keys layout was showing, looking just like a laptop keyboard, only with keys that were smaller than standard. Steve moved his eyes all over the iPad screen, rotating his head slowly in small figure eights, in what I took to be an attempt to get a view of every corner of the display, both straight on and in peripheral vision.

After several long moments of study, he reached out to tap the zoom key, triggering the beautifully crafted animation that Bas made to switch the keyboard to my bigger-keys design. No reaction, no hint of what he was thinking. Steve was like an expert high-stakes poker player checking his hole cards for the first time after receiving them from the dealer. Now that the screen looked different, Steve started his study all over again. He took his time, taking a solid thirty seconds to absorb every detail on the screen. Once satisfied, he tapped the zoom button again, returning the iPad to the more-keys layout. It now looked exactly as it had at the start of the demo. Steve studied again, still

betraying no sign of what he thought or felt. He tapped the zoom key one more time, changing to the bigger-keys layout again. He took in this view briefly, to confirm to himself that he had now seen the two designs, everything there was on offer. He turned to look straight at me.

"We only need one of these, right?"

Not what I was expecting. I think I may have swallowed hard. Steve was still looking at me, and so, with a half shrug, I said, "Yeah . . . uh . . . I guess so."

Steve sized me up a little and then asked, "Which one do you think we should use?"

A simple question, clearly directed at me and only me. Steve didn't shift in his chair or motion toward anyone else in the room. It was my demo, and he wanted me to answer.

And then something happened. Standing there, with Steve Jobs staring at me, waiting for me to respond to his question, I realized that I knew what to say, that I had an opinion.

"Well, I've been using these demos for the past few days, and I've started to like the keyboard layout with the bigger keys. I think I could learn to touch type on it, and I think other people could too. Autocorrection has been a big help."

Steve continued looking at me as he thought about my answer. He never moved his eyes to anyone or anything else. He was completely present. There he was, seriously considering my idea about the next big Apple product. It was thrilling. He thought for a few seconds about what I had just said and what he had seen on the iPad. Then he announced the demo verdict.

"OK. We'll go with the bigger keys."

That was it. The Oracle of Apple had spoken, the software design prophecy had been revealed, and with that, Steve gave a slight nod. The demo was over. Greg, Henri, and Bas stood up from their seats on the couch, and they offered a few encouraging comments like "Nice job" and "Good demo." I reverted to my natural state as an introvert, and having just received far more than my recommended daily dose of concentrated eye contact, I looked at the floor. The intensity in the room quickly dissipated. Scott walked a couple steps toward the door, giving the cue that it was time for me to go, so the rest of them could move on to whatever was next. I opened the door of Diplomacy. Scott followed behind me to close the door quietly, staying in the conference room as I left. I took one step out into the hallway and, just before the door latched shut, I heard Steve say, "Thank you."

* * *

Above the entrance to the Oracle at Delphi, there was a sign that read "Know Thyself," an admonition to questioners entering the shrine that the answers they were seeking inside might actually lie within. As I walked away from Diplomacy, I felt the satisfaction that I had known in the moment, and all by myself, what to say about my demo to Steve.

That was just the first impression I had about this demo after it was done, and I've thought much more about this meeting since then.

When Steve asked for my opinion, it was a test. After looking at my demo, he wanted to find out, right there, if I could help make the software better. If I hadn't given a satisfactory answer, he would have turned to the other people in the room. They had earned their places by repeatedly passing similar tests and making much work better, as on every software detail of the iPhone. If I wanted to keep presenting demos in Diplomacy—and I did, and I showed demos to Steve several more times in my career— making substantive contributions to the discussions with him was the way to earn future invitations.

For me, it would be the difference between writing software and influencing what software got written. In the case of this demo, my influence carried through, since the keyboard we shipped on the iPad was, barring a couple details like removing the now-unneeded zoom button, the same one I'd showed in my demo. I'd passed the test.

The relation of Diplomacy decision to shipping software also shows how important demos were to us at Apple. Demos served as the primary means to turn ideas into software. The setup of these demo review meetings reveals how we went about making our software great.

This statement includes the assumption that Apple made making great software an important goal to begin with. We did, and that came straight from Steve. He set the company's priorities, and he stressed, in public statements and internal communications, that making great software was a core corporate focus. What's more, Steve wasn't merely interested in paying lip service to this goal. He demanded action, and so the software team produced demos in a steady stream, and whenever there was interesting new work, Steve found the time to attend a demo review so he could see it. His involvement kept the progress and momentum going.

Given this equation of many demos leading to a single product, the five of us in Diplomacy there with Steve formed a key unit in the process—we were a team that could create an individual CEO-level demo. Between us, we had everything we needed. I was a programmer. Bas was a designer. Henri, Greg, and Scott were editors. In this collaboration, some of these roles could be fluid. Bas sometimes wrote bits of code, and often his demos went directly to Steve without the help of a programmer like me. In the case of this keyboard demo, I contributed some design thinking by adding a second keyboard with bigger keys.

Bas edited my choice of using the globe key to switch between the two keyboards I brought back to him.

Decisiveness was crucial throughout. At the pre-Steve level, Scott was the executive editor. He was the "decider." Every Apple demo review had a decider, the person with the sole authority to approve or not and the prerogative to declare what would happen next. Yet, even before formal reviews—say in a meeting between relatively experienced contributors like Bas and me—each of us could decide about our own portions of the work and whether we were willing to exert the effort and hours needed to pursue a new idea or make an additional refinement. Once we submitted work for a review with our team or with more junior people who were performing work on assignment, the team manager would be the decider. This practice continued on up the management chain. In particularly busy periods, Henri would hold his own demo reviews for all of iOS engineering, where he was the decider before Scott. The need to keep churning out demos that could eventually be shown to Steve meant our day-to-day software development work became a pyramid of demos, reviews, and decisions building up to the top and to Steve's final judgment.

Approving work wasn't the only decision to make. When Scott chose to bring me, and not just my demo, to the review with Steve, it was his way of saying that my word on the iPad keyboard counted as much as my work on it. He widened this circle around Steve only with care. From what I could tell, Steve judged him in part on whom he chose to bring. Such hierarchically restricted access to the CEO can't be too different from what happens with other large companies, but the way to get admission to these high-level meetings at Apple had much less to do with your place on the org chart and much more to do with your ability to make the products better. In those earlier instances when I handed over my iPhone keyboard prototypes to Henri for a Steve-level review I wouldn't be attending, it was hard for me to realize that my demo mattered to the company but my presence at the discussion about it didn't.

Scott also kept his job as demo gatekeeper for Steve because he advanced work only when it was of sufficiently high quality. Scott knew that he couldn't bring third-rate demos, with a claim that his team had toiled away on it assiduously, hoping to weasel his way to a CEO buy-off. That would have been a good way to trigger Steve's temper and a good way for Scott to lose his role as second-to-last decider. Scott also knew that he couldn't fix the demo procedure by trotting out the equivalent of one decently fast Thoroughbred mixed in with a bunch of old nags, expecting Steve would be happy he could pick the winner. Steve could see right through such ploys.

My demo was up to standard, the result of my collaboration with Bas. We had a solid proposal built on three strong components: two keyboards plus a way—a button and its animation—to stitch them together. Once in the review session with Steve, our efforts met with his editing. In our case, Steve saw something he liked, but he found the demo unnecessarily complicated, so he unpacked it. This deconstruction wasn't typical, but it was completely in character.

Even the discussion Steve used to arrive at his conclusion was spare and minimal. Note how Scott introduced my demo with just enough words to communicate to Steve what was next on the agenda, where he should turn his attention, and who I was. I, in turn, used the minimum number of words necessary to direct Steve's attention further, so he knew exactly what to look at. After that, Steve looked carefully at the software and asked me succinct questions to see if the work could be made simpler.

This push for simplicity had a purpose. Even though he was a high-tech CEO, Steve could put himself in the shoes of customers, people who cared nothing for the ins and outs of the software industry. He never wanted Apple software to overload people, especially when they might already be stretched by the bustle of their everyday lives.

Consider a mom who was busy with her daily routine, on a day she was worried about her sixteen-year-old son, who was home sick from high school and was taking care of himself. She was running a few minutes late getting to the office because there was bad traffic on the road, she had a report due later in the afternoon, and she was trying to fit in one more email reply as she headed down the hallway toward her next meeting.

Steve believed she'd do better with a product that wasn't loaded down with every thingamabob the product designers could dream up. He believed that stripping away nonessential features made products easier for people to learn from the start and easier to use over time. He wanted products and their software to speak for themselves. He realized that, in most cases, nobody would be standing over the shoulder of a person who is having their first experience with software, carefully describing every nuance of every feature. Sure, in a place like an Apple retail store, staff are always on hand to answer questions, but wouldn't it be better if software was clear and intuitive right off the bat?

Steve used demo reviews to judge for himself whether features met this basic usability standard. When he gave me the specific feedback to remove one of the two keyboards from my iPad demo, it had a cascade effect toward greater simplicity. It meant we could also take out the Bas zoom animation. We could also take away the zoom button. We could also take away possible confusion about which keyboard to show in different situations.

For example, should the software remember that you used the bigger-keys keyboard in the Notes app and the more-keys keyboard in Mail, and should these keyboard choices be restored in some situations but not in others? These questions became moot, and that's good, because they don't necessarily have easy answers. Steve figured that the best way to answer difficult questions like these was to avoid the need to ask them.

Steve's brand of decisiveness permeated Apple. He surrounded himself with people like Scott, Greg, Henri, and Bas at least in part because they could make good decisions without long deliberation. When Steve questioned me, it was a test of my decisiveness and whether I could make my demo better than it already was. Nobody else in the room chimed in because Steve was clearly looking to me, and the most efficient way of giving him the answer he was looking for was for me to speak up. I did, and he closed the loop on my demo.

Once Steve gave his verdict, everyone else knew it would have been foolhardy to argue with him, not because Steve wasn't open to contrary opinions but because doing so would mean speaking up in favor of adding back complexity. Hardly a winning hand. Scott, Henri, Greg, and Bas wouldn't have earned their place in Diplomacy unless they had a well-tuned sense of when it was best to say nothing. Bas never expressed any disappointment over his zoom animation getting deleted either. Seeing good work wind up on the cutting room floor was part of the job.

Demo reviews were also part of Steve's effort to model the product development behaviors he wanted us to use when he couldn't be present. As in Diplomacy, the whole software organization kept meetings and teams small to maintain efficiency and to reinforce the principle of doing the most with the least. Steve's constant demand to see a succession of demos spawned numerous other demos, each with their own presenters and deciders.

All these demos helped the entire software team stay focused on making great products.

This was all down to Steve. When he tacked on his "Thank you," it was his way of saying that my demo went just as he wanted. The meeting had been productive and decisive. It was a pattern to remember and replicate.

I chuckle to myself over how much time I've spent thinking about this iPad demo and how much Steve taught me in one meeting where he spoke just four sentences.

2

The Crystal Ball

Demos were fundamental to our work at Apple. We used them to highlight the potential, explore the concepts, show the progress, prompt the discussion, and drive the decisions for making our products. I started to understand how demos could play all these roles in creative and technical work when I was surprised by a single brilliant demo during my first few weeks at Apple, a moment that gave me my first real view into how the company made its software.

This "crystal ball" demo was set in the technology landscape of the early 2000s, a time when dot-com boom startups were still in business, Microsoft was the undisputed leader in computing, the Netscape web browser was the hottest new technology, and Apple was an underdog.

It was also a time when many Silicon Valley software companies started experimenting with free software and plans for turning a profit by developing software they wouldn't charge their customers to use. This seemingly paradoxical corporate strategy had its roots with Richard Stallman, a renowned programmer and technology activist, a man who believed *all* software should be free. Stallman railed against companies like Microsoft and Apple, which sold software for money, but kept the source code, the software instructions written by programmers, as a proprietary trade secret. In Stallman's idiosyncratic belief system, mixing computer code and the profit motive formed a toxic brew whose ill effects compelled companies to hoard the intellectual effort required to write programs and turned software development into a zero-sum game that impeded the advance of technology to the detriment of the human race. If you're not a programmer, free software might echo with sixties-style hippie idealism.

Yet *I am* a programmer, and for me, free software is more like the best candy store ever. If I picture myself as an entrepreneur with a dream of a new photo-sharing app, or a computer scientist researching artificial intelligence algorithms, or a system administrator trying to improve the utilization of the computers in my data center, I know I could go out on the internet and find existing code I could tailor for my own purpose. Free software made good solutions to common problems readily available, and in any of these scenarios, I could take advantage of free software as long as I allowed others to borrow from any code I wrote that was based on previously existing free software. Stallman positioned himself as the man behind the counter at the free software candy store, there not to ensure money changed hands but that the software source code would continue to change hands.

Stallman founded the GNU Project in 1983 to advocate for free software,[1] and he wrote the General Public License (GPL) to advance his agenda. Stallman calls the GPL a "copyleft," an intentionally contrasting reference to copyright, and rather than

restricting the privileges of software users, the GPL expands them, guaranteeing that everyone can get no-cost access to software source code and can study it, modify it, use it as is, or treat it the basis of new projects. This sounds free indeed, but the GPL had its catch. If you wrote software based on code covered by the GPL, you were required to publish your software under the GPL as well. The expectation was that this would create a virtuous cycle in which coders were continuously building on each other's efforts to the betterment of all, rich or poor, newbie or geek, programmer or end user.

If you don't work in the software industry, Richard Stallman might be one of the most influential people you've never heard of. Over the decades, free software has spread through the entire high-tech industry. His GPL drives the development of the Linux operating system, and Linux is the core software running on Android smartphones, in the data centers for Google, Amazon, Twitter, and Facebook, and on the majority of network servers of all kinds. Without the long-term influence of Stallman's ideas and all the free software inspired by them, the internet as we know it would not exist. There would likely be no web search engines, streaming music, or YouTube. No Wikipedia either. No chat apps. No social networks. No smartphones. The world would be a different place.

My life would be different too. Before coming to Apple, I had a job at a startup called Eazel. Our goal was to create an easy-to-use Linux system suitable for everyday computing, a free software alternative to Apple Macintosh and Microsoft Windows. The company was led by programmers who worked on the original Macintosh in the 1980s, including Bud Tribble, the first software manager for the Mac, and Andy Hertzfeld, the software wizard whose graphical user interface code helped to set the Mac apart from the text-mode personal computers that were the norm of the time. These fellows were my heroes, and I joined the company to work with them. The elegance and simplicity of their Mac software was my main inspiration for wanting to become a programmer.[2]

The inspiration for Eazel came from Andy, and his vision for the company was fueled by the free software movement—Andy identified with Stallman's idealism—and by his concept of developing a file and icon manager that would make Linux a fitting competitor to Windows and the Mac, its more established rivals. Andy called this program Nautilus, and it would help Eazel users find files, read email, launch programs like word processors and spreadsheets, and perhaps do cool new things like keeping track of a few digital photos. Eazel contributed Nautilus to the GNOME project, a loosely confederated free software community whose members, both individuals and companies, would be providing the rest of the software for the desktop computing system we were trying to build.

To be a part of GNOME, Nautilus had to be licensed under the GPL. This had important implications for Eazel as a commercial entity. Since people would be able to download Nautilus for free once we finished it, the company had to figure out some other way to make money. Not surprisingly, this involved creating proprietary software that Eazel could charge people to use: a set of proto-cloud services, including automatic software updates and online file storage. These cloud services would live in an Eazel data center and would not be free. The idea was to integrate Nautilus with these services and position our no-cost software as a lure to draw people to Eazel's pay-to-use features. The combination of dot-com fervor, enthusiasm over Linux and free software, abundant venture capital money, and our founders' connection to the Mac made it seem to me that Eazel might be the next big thing.

If indeed we had that chance, we fumbled it. We never lived up to any of our lofty goals. Chief among our missteps was failing to conceive of our software as a single product instead of as a set of separate projects. We never figured out how to integrate the pieces. Nothing worked smoothly. Our software update feature was riddled with bugs that often broke programs while trying to update them. Our code to connect Nautilus to our cloud services didn't work at all. The Nautilus team had persistent problems coordinating with GNOME—the loose structure and lack of profit motive of the free software community meant that they did not share our money-making goals or care to coordinate with us so we could meet our delivery schedules. All these setbacks caused delay after delay.

Several months into my stint at the company, these problems were becoming unavoidable, and our management went looking for help to whip our software into shape. One Friday afternoon, I sat in my office cubicle waiting to meet the man who might provide it. Earlier that week, I'd noticed "Don Moulton" scrawled on a piece of paper taped up in an empty cubicle near mine—he would be starting the following Monday as manager of the Nautilus project. That evening I met Don for the first time at one of our monthly shindigs. He promptly noted that some "knucklehead" had spelled his name wrong. He walked me over to his cube and scrawled over the scrawling: Don MELTON.

Don had some geek street cred, stemming from the several appearances he'd made in *Code Rush,* a documentary that aired on PBS.[3] This film recounted the "browser wars," the struggle between Netscape and Microsoft to control the early days of web surfing. As more and more people discovered the internet in the 1990s, Microsoft began to fear that computer users would change their technology habits, shifting money and influence to Netscape, the company that made the most popular web browser.

Microsoft attempted to squish Netscape by bundling its own web browser, Internet Explorer, with its Windows operating system, then used on well over 90 percent of personal computers. Microsoft expected this move would cut off any opportunity for Netscape to cash in on the appeal and reach of its browser, reasoning that few people would go looking for a browser if they already had Internet Explorer preinstalled on their computer.

All of a sudden, Netscape needed a new strategy if it hoped to remain relevant in the web browser market it helped to create. As its countermove, Netscape decided to publish its browser source code, in the hope that the freely available code might become the de facto standard for all internet-enabled apps. If it did, this might lead to technical support contracts, consulting deals, and other ways of making money not directly tied to web browsers.

This "open source" strategy was a variation inspired by the free software movement but one Richard Stallman didn't favor. Stallman wanted code to be free as a political and social good. His notion was for software to be "free as in freedom."[4] For Netscape, open source was an attempt to save the company from going under. It was making its source code "free as in beer."[5] The hope was to earn money by running the best beer bash.

History has shown this didn't work, and while Netscape didn't survive as a stand-alone company, it did ship the open source version of its browser code, christened with a new name: Mozilla. Mozilla had made it out the door with much thanks to Don, my new Eazel colleague, since he was responsible for purging all the dirty words from the source code before it was released.

That rude language was a hurdle Netscape needed to clear in its open-source initiative provides a peek into the inner workings of software development culture. Even as I write, but perhaps more so in the early 2000s, programmers are predominantly youngish men just a few years out of college, geeks who gulp caffeine to fuel long hours of coding, often against impossibly tight delivery schedules. When tired and short on time, tempers flare, immaturity clobbers professionalism, and disputes, technical or otherwise, come out in the software. Using the camel case scheme programmers often favor to mash together several words into one, a representative example of inappropriate language in source code might be:

```
cleanUpBobsSh_tStormHeIsAF__kingTurdBlossom();
```

Fearing that such bad language might harm the appeal of its software once the source was opened up and anyone could see it, Netscape management issued a decree: All the programming profanity would have to go. Cleaning up the code was a big task. Don was tapped to get it done, and he would say he was the goddamn perfect man for the job. He had a pretty foul mouth himself. He found and fixed up all the dirty language, but open source didn't substantially improve Netscape's fate in the browser wars. It lost.

As impending defeat was becoming clear, Don decided to look elsewhere for work. By the time he joined us at Eazel, software delays weren't our only problem. Money was getting tight. Eazel had no products to sell, and our previous round of funding was running out. Our executives were busy trying to secure more investment, and for a while, they gave the Eazel staff updates every few weeks. Then they went quiet. Too quiet.

Fast forward a couple months: No venture capitalist had written a check, and on the same day Eazel shipped Nautilus 1.0, the company fired two-thirds of its staff. Don and I were in the smaller group who held on for three more months as our execs tried to sell the company outright, but to no avail.

Don and I were out of a job, but we had become friends, and when we weren't strolling the fairways at several Silicon Valley golf courses, we looked for work. We soon heard that Apple was hiring. The Cupertino computer company held a job fair for former Eazel employees. I scored a couple of business cards from managers and planned to follow up. But Don, who was always more clever than me at pulling levers, had another idea. The next thing I knew, I had an interview with Scott Forstall, then the director of Platform Experience at Apple. In the days before iPods and iPhones, this was the department responsible for the Mac's user interface, system apps like Finder and Mail, as well as the software frameworks that third-party developers used to make their own Mac programs.

When I arrived for my interview on the Apple campus, I found Scott sitting at his desk, which was angled into the far corner of his office. When I walked in, he swiveled around and leaned forward in his chair like a prizefighter waiting for the next round to begin. I sat knees to knees with him as we exchanged introductions. Since I had been worried ahead of time about my interviewing skills, I brought along a prop, my latest unemployed-guy software project, a jigsaw puzzle app that ran on Mac OS X, Apple's brand-new operating system.

Scott tried my app, seemed to like it, and then peppered me with questions about my software with a speed and sting reminiscent of a youthful Muhammad Ali throwing a flurry of left-right combinations.

"How did you design the algorithm to make new puzzle pieces?"

"What technique did you use to make your animations so smooth?"

"Did you choose Cocoa or Carbon frameworks or some combination?"

The interview was a fast-paced blur, and I struggled to keep up. I later learned that Scott was always like this. You had to be on your guard, or his fusillade of questions might knock you off your feet.

A couple days later, Don and I drove over to the Computer Literacy bookshop in Sunnyvale—he said he wanted to pick up a book. I tried to get him to tell me about his interview at Apple and if he'd gotten any feedback about mine with Scott, but he stonewalled. When we left the store and got back in his car, Don handed me a copy of *JavaScript: The Definitive Guide, 3rd Edition*, notable for the beautifully detailed rhinoceros on its cover.[6]

He said, "What do you think about making a web browser for Apple? Are you interested?"

I was.

But wait a minute. Didn't Mac OS X have a web browser? Yes, it did. Microsoft Internet Explorer. A deal between Apple and Microsoft had brought Internet Explorer to the Mac four years earlier. Steve Jobs announced this arrangement in August 1997, on the same day he invited Bill Gates to appear by video feed during his keynote at the Macworld Expo held in Boston.[7] On that day, Gates pledged Microsoft's support for Apple, committed to ship Office for Mac for five years, invested $150 million in Apple, and agreed to furnish Internet Explorer to Apple as the default web browser on the Mac. Except for the unfortunate optics of a twenty-foot-high Bill Gates looming over a Mac conference hall like Big Brother, it was a good deal for Apple, a welcome vote of confidence at a time when many were predicting the company's impending doom. A few months earlier, *Wired* had published its famous cover image of the multicolor Apple logo encircled by barbed wire. A one-word caption below read: Pray.[8]

By the summer of 2001, Apple was on firmer footing, buoyed by the completion of Mac OS X, the success of the iMac, and the (secret) hopes for the iPod, which would be released four months later.

Steve and Scott were keen to keep this momentum going, and since they believed the internet would be an important part of the future of computing, communication, and commerce, they wanted Apple to control its own destiny in this burgeoning technology domain. They wanted the flexibility to improve the company's internet software at will, and having an in-house browser was the first step in this strategy. They slated Microsoft Internet Explorer for replacement.

On the day Don and I joined Apple, this browser replacement initiative became our job. It involved two interlocking goals. First, make a web browser app. Second, create a web technology toolkit that would make it easy for Apple's third-party software developers to incorporate web features into their software, from downloading text and images to displaying entire web pages. Simple to say, and indeed, web browsers do seem simple from the point of view of using one to surf the web.

From the perspective of a programmer, web browsers are fiendishly complicated. Since I had never worked on one before, Don held a mini boot camp to bring me up to speed. During our 7 a.m. coffee runs to the on-campus café every day, he'd run through a web browser's major subsystems: content (text and images), styling (fonts, colors, and placement), and scripting (dynamic behaviors like checking a form before you submit it). He told me about the alphabet soup of published standards to cover these respective technical areas: Hypertext Markup Language (HTML), Cascading Style Sheets (CSS), and the JavaScript programming language. He also described how these software pieces fit together to produce complex web pages.

As I listened and learned, it seemed like making a browser would be a tall order for two people, especially when Don mentioned the large teams Netscape had working on its browser. No doubt Microsoft had the same for Internet Explorer. We would be a team of two. How could we possibly compete?

Don told me not to worry. We had a trick up our sleeve. We wouldn't be starting from scratch, as had been done at a web-browsing pioneer like Netscape. As a result of the free software movement and the browser wars, Netscape had published its source code for Mozilla. This meant Don and I could turn to open source. We could download and evaluate the software at any level of detail we desired, and the Mozilla license meant we could borrow their code for our project.

Several other open source web browser projects were available on the internet, and we put investigations of these other projects on our to-do list. There were a couple commercially available options to assess as well. Even with these due diligence plans, Mozilla was our leading candidate right away, mostly because of Don's connection to that code. He expressed confidence we could leverage the work of those big teams at Netscape. Yet as we talked, I realized that Don had a love/hate relationship with Mozilla. On the upside, Mozilla represented a huge investment in web technology, so we could use it to avoid having to reinvent the wheel at Apple. The downside was that the source code base was hard to work with because it was huge, many times larger than the software Don and I had collaborated on at Eazel. Given Don's technical introduction sessions, I just accepted that web browsers needed to be super-big programming projects, and I got used to the idea that I'd need to understand all this new code.

Indeed, when I downloaded Mozilla from the internet, my first impression of the source code was its sheer size—close to a million and a half lines. I had never before worked on a project even a quarter as large. Printed at thirty lines to a page, the Mozilla code would fill fifty thousand pages. Imagine being compelled to read a stack of books that tall and then submit to an exam that might ask about any arbitrary line.

Regardless, that was the job, and I figured I'd better start studying. I moved in for a closer look at the software, but I immediately hit a roadblock. Mozilla wouldn't "build" on Mac OS X, meaning that while I had all the programming source code for the Mozilla browser, when I tried to turn the code into an app that would run on Apple's three-month-old operating system, it wouldn't work. Apparently, nobody knowledgeable with Mozilla had ever tried. The Mac's paltry market share was biting us. I searched the internet for help, but I didn't find anything useful, and since our project was a secret, I couldn't post questions to online message boards, as programmers often do, or even ask any of my new colleagues inside Apple. After a few days of build failures, I declared myself stuck.

I had been reporting my lack of progress to Don, who had been spending his time in secret negotiations with closed source vendors who might be willing to license their browser code to Apple. Don still preferred Mozilla, an open source solution, mostly because he believed free software would be an easier "sell" to our management than the multimillion-dollar price tag on the commercial alternatives.

Meanwhile, the higher-ups at Apple were eagerly awaiting for word from us, a recommendation, a sign of progress, something to show we were making headway. I would later find out that Scott was beginning to have his doubts about us. I'm glad I didn't know, because after a month of treading water, I was already starting to feel the pressure on my own.

Don and I huddled. He said he was going out for a week of vacation he'd planned before we got to Apple. He wanted me to spend the week holed up in an all-out effort to build Mozilla on Mac OS X.

I dug in. I took meticulous notes. I spent long hours with the code. When Don got back to the office, I handed him a document entitled *Building the Lizard: Fifty Steps to Get Mozilla Running on Mac OS X.*

Each step was critical. Some steps seemed whacko, especially the one, about halfway down the list, to rebuild a piece of my programming environment, the C language library, a requirement that was the software equivalent of a brain transplant. It made *Building the Lizard* seem less like a technical document and more like a diabolical script from a low-budget monster movie.

The good news was that these steps worked . . . sort of. By following the directions, I could produce a web browser program icon on my desktop. The bad news was that this Frankenstein version of an app wasn't alive. When I double-clicked this icon with my mouse, Mozilla launched, but it wouldn't load web pages—whenever I tried, the browser promptly crashed. As I set out to investigate, I became hopelessly tangled in the million-plus lines of source code.

While we were conducting these browser evaluations, we were also trying to hire other people to join the team. We'd been approved to hire a couple more programmers, and even before our official Apple start date, we had spent time recruiting. Don knew several people from Netscape with browser-building experience, we knew some excellent engineers from Eazel who still hadn't decided on their next job, and we got a couple leads on Apple-internal candidates. We faced a new challenge too: trying to convince people who had good alternatives to take a job on a project that we couldn't tell them about. Don's approach was a wink combined with assurance that it was a "big job." Everyone turned us down. The ones with previous experience at Netscape took the unstated hint from Don, and none wanted any part of making another browser. My recent difficulties with Mozilla gave me an inkling about why they felt that way.

Now, in the midst of my efforts to tame Mozilla, I met another candidate. Richard Williamson began by telling me that he knew how to get results fast. In his British-accented English, tempered by two decades in the United States, he told me about himself. He had started his own software company when in his early teens, attended Swarthmore for a couple years, then paused his studies to work a year at NeXT, Steve Jobs's inter-Apple software company. After returning to NeXT upon graduating, he sometimes fielded requests directly from The Man, like the time Steve sent him to Japan to negotiate with a partner to build an add-on networking card for NeXT computers, which he did successfully.

Richard delivered every word with confidence, and he seemed to have the experience to back it up. He and I were the same age, but I'd been playing computer games at the time he founded his first software company. In his early twenties, he'd brokered a multinational deal for NeXT in Japan. I was in the country too, teaching English, just another long-haired guy with a recently minted college degree and a duffel bag.

But was Richard for real, or was he just a smooth talker? As I tried to decide, I asked him about specific technical problems he faced and how he tackled them. Each time he recounted another quick-to-find solution. I also noticed that he punctuated all his answers by sticking out the index finger and pinky on each hand at about shoulder width, tips pointed at each other. Then he'd bring his hands together, randomly rotating his forearms as he did so. When his hands meshed directly in front of him, he rotated his forearms again, but this time in sync with each other, evoking the image of a motor delivering power through a drive shaft and onto its wheels. After every question I asked, he'd do it again, as if to show me that, for him, creating software was as simple as this drive shaft gesture.

After the interview, I went to Don and told him I wasn't sure what to make of Richard's bold claims. Don said that Bertrand Serlet, Scott Forstall's boss, had worked with Richard at NeXT and spoke very highly of him. Don had been impressed during their interview and wanted to hire him. But he respected my reservations, and he suggested I call Richard on the phone for another chat.

This follow-up call was just like our face-to-face interview. Richard gave the same confident answers, and I pictured him holding the phone to his ear with his shoulder so he could do the two-handed drive shaft gesture. When I hung up the phone, I still wasn't sure, but I had no concrete objections, so I gave Don my thumbs-up. Richard would be the third member of our team.

Richard started at Apple during my second week struggling to make Mozilla do more than build, launch, and crash. On his first day, Don and I gave him a full update on everything we had done, our open source strategy, Don's discussions with outside companies, a listing of the candidate browser source code options we had considered, our decision to focus on Mozilla, my *Building the Lizard* document, and the bolts-protruding-from-the-neck, crash-prone hulk of a browser produced by following those steps.

Richard asked, "How long have you guys been working on this browser project?" His tone indicated that he wasn't impressed.

Don answered, "Six weeks."

Richard scrunched up his face in confusion at our lack of progress. He launched into a series of technical questions,

delving into details. Was he trying to identify some valuable nugget we had missed? As we went on, it seemed Richard was too polite to ask the question really on his mind: "What on earth have you guys been doing?"

Later on, when Don and I had a chance to chat by ourselves, we concluded that Richard simply didn't understand how hard this browser project was going to be. That would soon change. We agreed that we liked our new teammate, and we could look past any gruff behavior because it was accompanied by an eagerness to get going. We'd give Richard a week or so to get his computer and office set up, then we would talk to him about the project some more.

It didn't take Richard that long to get settled in. Two days later, he called us over to take a look at a demo. A what? A demo?

Don and I walked into Richard's dark, windowless office, a room lit only by the screen of his Mac. We looked over his shoulder as Richard clicked his mouse and launched a web browser. Not just the shell of one, but an actual functioning web browser. He proceeded to load web pages, click links, go back, click more links, load more pages, and generally surf the web like it was no big deal. What the hell were we looking at?

He explained that we were looking at Konqueror, one of the open source browsers *we* had told *him* about a couple days earlier. Konqueror had been developed by KDE, a programming community with goals similar to the GNOME project we'd favored at Eazel. KDE also was a full-featured computing environment, similar to Mac and Windows, a system built around the free software core of Linux.

Richard said he'd downloaded KDE and set himself a simple goal: Get the code running on the Mac as quickly as possible so he could evaluate the potential of the Konqueror web browser.

Since KDE ran on Linux, not on Mac OS X, Richard told us he'd made a shim, a software translation layer that tricked the Konqueror browser into thinking it was running on a Linux computer, and then cajoled the computer into believing the browser was a program custom-tailored to the Mac. To be clear: Writing a shim like this is incredibly difficult. To have considered the task as less than an impassable technical roadblock was extraordinary. To see this shim working in just two days proved that Richard's self-confidence was well founded. We were looking at a programming tour-de-force.

Sensing our wonder, Richard told us about the two shortcuts he'd taken to make his demo work. First, he'd used the Linux graphical system, X Windows, rather than Apple Core Graphics, the system native to Mac OS X. Second, he was running the entire KDE system, not just the Konqueror web browser. Even if these items might sound like technical mumbo jumbo to you, they didn't to us, and as Richard described his work further, Don and I began to see how these shortcuts had allowed him to get the Konqueror code up and running fast.

Richard didn't worry that X Windows failed to integrate perfectly with the top-of-screen menu bar on the Mac or provide pixel-perfect font rendering, or that the full KDE system included a raft of software that was irrelevant to web browsing. Richard knew these technical details would need to be addressed down the road, but he also knew how unease about his shortcuts would melt away in the minds of the demo viewer as soon as he turned back to his computer and continued surfing the web in what looked very much like a Mac browser.

Indeed, the unease did melt away, and with his caveats disclosed, that was it. Just a shim, two clever shortcuts, and two days to produce a working browser demo. Richard's quick results were evidence of a deep vein of potential in Konqueror, one we could explore, mine, and exploit.

Don and I had been working for six weeks on our new job of making a web browser for the Mac, but we still had no working code to show for it and no plan for how we would produce any. In a fraction of the time, Richard had downloaded a Linux web browser and had coaxed Konqueror into running on his Mac. His demo browser launched, it loaded web pages, it didn't crash, and it performed smoothly. Don and I were amazed. If Richard had done his two-handed drive shaft gesture, I think I might have fainted.

How did Richard pull this off? Both Don and I were experienced engineers, and Don had spent years developing web browsers at Netscape, yet Richard's demo caught us completely off guard.

Is it possible to understand his accomplishment better, to measure it, to quantify it? It's tempting to cite Silicon Valley lore and call Richard a "10x programmer," a super-productive software genius who can add value in multiples of mere mortals.[9]

Do such people exist? After all, such discontinuities between average and excellent are uncommon in everyday life. The person sitting at the next table in a coffee shop won't be typing five hundred words per minute on his or her laptop keyboard while you sit at yours typing fifty. The physical world imposes hard limits. This remains true even at elite levels of human performance. No Olympic sprinter will ever cover the 100 meters in less than one second.

Do these kinds of limits extend to technology development? In his 1975 software engineering classic, *The Mythical Man Month,* Frederick P. Brooks Jr. says that they do. Sharing the lessons he learned while managing the OS/360 mainframe operating system project at IBM in the 1960s, Brooks offers this observation:

"When a task cannot be partitioned because of sequential constraints, the application of more effort has no effect on the schedule. The bearing of a child takes nine months, no matter how many women are assigned."[10]

But do these limits *always* apply in software development? In the large projects Brooks was speaking about, where teams of hundreds or thousands are working against schedules and initiatives with mutual dependencies, the size of the effort bounds the speed of the work, and the overhead of communication and coordination swamps the impact of individuals, even the geniuses.

However, in the early phase of software development, it's possible to shake free of these restrictions, especially when teams are small and the hunt for ideas is still on. This was the scenario when Richard joined us at Apple. We were still looking for an organizing concept to kick-start our web browser effort, and Richard showed us how. Not only that, he proved that a 10x productivity gap is a conservative upper limit on the possible in early stage software. Indeed, Richard did more to move our project ahead in two person-days of work than Don and I had done in the preceding twelve person-weeks. That's more like a 30x gap.

What can explain this difference? On the surface, much appears to hinge on Richard's programming feat, his software shim. Otherwise, his effort with Konqueror seems much like my struggles with Mozilla. Perhaps he was just a better programmer than me, and without his coding cleverness, there would be no story.

That explanation is too simple. Richard made his shim only after determining he needed one last link in a chain of inspiration, intuition, reasoning, and estimation. His shim was a consequence of his overall plan. To show what I mean, here's an accounting of what Richard did in his first couple of days at Apple.

He began by quizzing us on the browser analysis we had done before his arrival, and after hearing it, he quickly discarded our effort with Mozilla as unlikely to bear fruit. By doing so, he demonstrated the self-confidence to skip any ingratiating display of deference to his new manager, a person who had years of experience in the technical field he was newly entering. Next, Richard resolved to produce a result on the shortest possible schedule. He downloaded an open source project that held genuine promise, the Konqueror code from KDE, a browser that might well serve as the basis for our long-term effort. In getting this code running on a Mac, he decided to make the closest possible approximation of a real browser that was feasible on his short schedule. He identified three features—loading web pages, clicking links, and going back to previous pages. He reasoned these alone would be sufficiently compelling proofs of concept. He then made his shortcuts, and these simplifying choices defined a set of nongoals: Perfect font rendering would be cast aside, as would full integration with the Mac's native graphics system, same for using only the minimum source code from KDE. He reasoned that these shortcuts, while significant, would not substantially detract from the impact of seeing a browser surf web pages. He resolved to draw together these strands into a single demo that would show the potential of Konqueror. Then, finally, he worked through the technical details, which led him to develop his software shim, since that was the only thing standing between him and the realization of his plan. His thought process amplified his technical acumen.

In contrast, Don and I were hoping Mozilla would pan out somehow. I was trying to get the open source behemoth to build on the Mac, with little thought beyond that. I had no comparable plan, goals, nongoals, tight schedule, or technical shortcuts.

More than anything, this difference in thinking led to the difference in our outcomes. It's not that Don and I were in a temporary rut either. Our approach at Apple was much similar to the one we used at Eazel, where we never had any idea whether we were on track to deliver an excellent desktop-plus-proto-cloud service for the simple reason that we were never able to try out our software in an integrated form until days before our company ran out of money and laid off most of its staff. At Eazel, we had never considered anything like the quick get-it-done schemes Richard just showed us.

If Don and I had continued working in the Eazel way at Apple, who knows when we would have had a demo to show? At that point in our careers, we simply didn't know how to bootstrap a big project and set it on a course for success.

Richard did. His demo was the lynchpin. He showed us that the Konqueror web browser could work on the Mac. He cut corners to highlight the potential of this code. Of course, Richard's brilliant software shim made his breakthrough possible, but consider the conceptual framework he'd built around his plan and how he'd cornered all the difficulties of making a browser demo so that one piece of custom programming, his shim, was all that was left to close the circle. The cumulative effect created the illusion of a real browser even when only showing an incomplete portion of one.

And it worked. When Don and I saw this demo, it was as if Richard had called us into his office, set a crystal ball down on the table, waved his hand over it, and showed us a vision for the future of our web browser project, one that pointed the way to make the vision real.

Richard's demo also points to some general lessons, and to describe what they are, I'll turn to an industry with a long history of using simplifying choices and corner cutting—some of the same tricks Richard used in his demo—to make us see things that aren't really there.

Consider Hollywood backlots, the semipermanent outdoor locations movie studios maintain on their properties, the sidewalks, alleyways, and main streets that filmmakers employ as settings for their stories. Especially in decades past, before expensive location shoots and computer-aided special effects became common, backlots were essential. Even on a shoestring budget, a backlot could transform a scene. However, for the illusion to be convincing to moviegoers, we must see the correct amount of replicated reality onscreen.

One of my favorite backlot scenes is from *Singin' in the Rain*, the 1952 Metro-Goldwyn-Mayer musical starring Gene Kelly and Debbie Reynolds. Take the eponymous dance number in the film—where Gene Kelly jubilantly taps, jumps, splashes, and spins his way through the pouring rain after he kisses Debbie Reynolds good night on the doorstep of her apartment. This scene is set on a Hollywood backlot intended to look like a city street. Immediately before Kelly dunks himself under a gushing downspout draining water from the roofs of the "buildings" he is dancing past, he skips past La Valle Millinery Shop, an enticing-looking storefront with several fashionable women's hats on display. Of course, this wasn't a real shop. The storefront might have been a cobbled-together flat with nothing behind it, or there might have been a studio office through the "shop" door, perhaps for an MGM bookkeeper or clerk. We don't care. We're too charmed by the singing and dancing. Compare this fake hat shop with another prop seen earlier in the number, when Kelly jumps up on a lamppost on the edge of the sidewalk. Unlike the hat shop, that lamppost prop needed to be real, or at least real enough to support the actor's weight. Were other lampposts on the backlot similarly well built? We don't know, but again, we

don't care. Maybe they were, and maybe they weren't, but the set designers needed to make sure that one specific lamppost was sufficiently sturdy for the movie's lead character to leap up onto it. It had to be built well because the choreography called for it.

In the same way, software demos need to be convincing enough to explore an idea, to communicate a step toward making a product, even though the demo is not the product itself. Like the movie, demos should be specifically choreographed, so it's clear what must be included and what can be left out. Those things that aren't the main focus of a demo, but are required to create the proper setting, must be realized at the correct level of detail so they contribute to the whole rather than detract from the vision.

Richard put this theory into practice. He chose the Konqueror open source browser as the basis of his work, one of the candidates we might use for the actual product, and he ensured he could load web pages, click links, and go back. Those aspects were essential. The font rendering was not to Apple standards—some characters were jaggy rather than smooth—but text was legible enough, so Richard expended no more effort on typography. He spent no time at all on irrelevant details, like keyboard shortcuts or a beautifully designed app icon. He chose this combination of important/passable/ignorable features carefully to maximize impact, minimize distractions, and fit the work schedule he'd set for himself.

In the years since Richard showed me his browser demo, I've emulated his approach. When I make a demo, I think about the intended audience, and I make a specific decision about what outside the ring other less important details that will eventually have to be addressed, but not immediately. I pay them as little attention as possible. Like the inside of the hat shop, I omit them from the demo if I can get away with it. I take extra care at the boundary. Some elements are right on the thick imaginary line, details that need some attention, since they help to set the scene and get my audience to suspend their disbelief. In the case of a preferences screen, a minor user interface element for an app still in early development, I might take a screenshot from the preferences of another app rather than implement a fully working user interface. This is similar to placing a few hat props in the shop window. I want my demo audience to think they're looking at something real, even though they aren't. I know the demo isn't an actual product, and my audience knows it too, but creating the illusion of an actual product is essential during the development process to maintain the vision of what we're actually trying to achieve, and so my colleagues can begin responding and giving feedback as if the demo was the product.

This attempt to build continuity throughout a development process suggests one final characteristic shared between backlot scenes and software demos—both are elements in larger narratives. Each advances its story. Gene Kelly's dancing and singing in the rain expresses the joy of a first kiss, the moment in the film when the leading man and woman show us that they've fallen for each other. It was Hollywood movie magic at its best. Richard's demo was the moment we saw the potential of the Konqueror open source code and decided it might be the answer we had been looking for. It was Silicon Valley software magic at its best.

Over time, Don and I began to understand and absorb the model Richard showed us. Look for ways to make quick progress. Watch for project stalls that might indicate a lack of potential. Cut corners to skip unnecessary effort. Remove distractions to focus attention where it needs to be. Start approximating your end goal as soon as possible. Maximize the impact of your most difficult effort. Combine inspiration, decisiveness, and craft to make demos.

We learned all this from Richard. He changed the way we worked.

3

The Black Slab

Right after we saw Richard's demo, there was much we still didn't know about Konqueror, the open source web browser, but we were eager to find out if was as good as it seemed. Don suggested we take a closer look at the source code itself, the body of programmer-written instructions that made the software what it was. Specifically, Don wanted us to start isolating Konqueror from the rest of KDE—to begin uncutting one of the corners Richard had cut to make his demo. He also wanted to get an estimate on Konqueror's complexity, so we decided to count the number of lines in its source code. This count would give us both a means of comparison to Mozilla and some idea for how hard it might be to turn Richard's demo into a real product.

Don gave this line counting job to me, possibly as a way of getting me invested in the success of Richard's impressive programming feat. If that was the case, it worked. The morning after the demo, I got to the office about an hour earlier than usual, around 6 a.m. On my desk, next to my Mac, I set up a PC tower computer. My plan was to install Linux on this PC and download all the KDE source code onto it. Once that was done, I would scan through the code and run some tests to begin separating Konqueror from the system surrounding it.

While I waited for various installation steps to finish, I looked at the two computers in front of me: a Linux PC and a Mac. They were separated from each other on my desk by only a few inches, but the software gap loomed large. Although Linux and Mac OS X traced a common software lineage extending back to UNIX, an operating system created as a research project at Bell Laboratories in 1969, both had diverged significantly from that shared ancestor. Over time, Linux and Mac had become like two different countries separated by the same language. Linux said "lorry" where the Mac said "truck." When it came to end user apps like web browsers, the compatibilities between them were narrow, but deeper down, at the algorithmic level where we worked as programmers, the resemblances between the two systems were broader. They retained some common technical grammar and syntax, and both systems could build and run programs written in C++, the programming language the Konqueror developers used to write their source code. Even so, Linux and Mac used different programming vocabularies and idioms for expressing programs in C++, especially when it came to graphical user interfaces. The net result was we couldn't just copy the code from one computer to the other. If we wanted to use Konqueror as the basis of our web browser project, we would have to patch up all such terminology and technology differences in Konqueror's Linux source code and replace Richard's shim with solid software engineering. Adapting the code written for one operating system so that it works on another is common enough that programmers have a word to describe the task: porting. Since we could deliver an Apple-quality web browser only from source code that worked like it was written natively for the Mac—even though it wasn't—our porting job would have to be very good indeed.

It didn't take me long to isolate the web browser code in the KDE system. The software had a tidy organization, and Konqueror lived primarily in two directories: one called KHTML, the other KJS.

After I separated them out, I asked the computer to count the total number of lines in these two directories. This would give a rough indication of how big our porting effort would be. Since each line of code might need some porting work, the fewer lines, the better. When I saw the result, I smiled, and when I shared this number with Don and Richard, they smiled too. At just over 120,000 lines, Konqueror was less than one-tenth the size of Mozilla.[1] At first, we couldn't believe there could be such a difference between two bodies of source code that performed the same function.

Don explained. The Mozilla project leaders had designed a system they hoped would turn their software into components they could snap together like LEGOs. However, this scheme required reams of extra boilerplate code—programmers had to do something like filling out a pile of forms to register new code with this reuse system—and this buried their browser in red tape. Now that we saw the implications of this engineering decision and the resulting 10:1 ratio of Mozilla code to Konqueror code, it seemed obvious that their component notion had gotten wildly out of hand. Mozilla was bloated, unwieldy, and troublesome.

The Konqueror team had taken the opposite tack. Their code was lean and lithe. They prized brevity. Their software style

Konqueror, and my postdemo analysis of source code lines had taken just a couple hours. This didn't mean our porting effort would be a walk in the park, but we liked how quickly these early successes with Konqueror had come.

This gave us the confidence to commit. Don said he would team with Richard to show his demo up the software engineering management chain. The hope was to get buy-in from Scott Forstall, from his boss Bertrand Serlet, and his boss Avie Tevanian, that we should use Konqueror as the basis of our web browser project.

Fast forward a few days, and the executives were as amazed as we'd hoped. Richard's demo was so clear and compelling that no cajoling was necessary to convince management that our browser project was now on track.

With their approval, our next step was to develop a strategy for porting those 120,000 lines of Konqueror code to the Mac. Understanding the complicated piece of programming we were about to attempt requires a little knowledge of software development jargon.

* * *

When I want a computer to perform a job, I type out my precise instructions using a programming language, like C++, the language the KDE developers used to write Konqueror.

These statements are probably unintelligible if you're unfamiliar with the notation programmers use to write code, but

```
/*
    Copyright (C) 2001 Apple Computer, Inc.  All rights reserved.

    Redistribution and use in source and binary forms, with or without modification, are permitted
    provided that the following conditions are met:

    1. Redistributions of source code must retain the above copyright notice, this list of
    conditions and the following disclaimer.
    2. Redistributions in binary form must reproduce the above copyright notice, this list of
    conditions and the following disclaimer in the documentation and/or other materials provided
    with the distribution.

    THIS SOFTWARE IS PROVIDED BY APPLE COMPUTER, INC. ``AS IS'' AND ANY EXPRESS OR IMPLIED
    WARRANTIES, INCLUDING, BUT NOT LIMITED TO, THE IMPLIED WARRANTIES OF MERCHANTABILITY AND
    FITNESS FOR A PARTICULAR PURPOSE ARE DISCLAIMED.  IN NO EVENT SHALL APPLE COMPUTER, INC. OR
    CONTRIBUTORS BE LIABLE FOR ANY DIRECT, INDIRECT, INCIDENTAL, SPECIAL, EXEMPLARY, OR
    CONSEQUENTIAL DAMAGES (INCLUDING, BUT NOT LIMITED TO, PROCUREMENT OF SUBSTITUTE GOODS OR
    SERVICES; LOSS OF USE, DATA, OR PROFITS; OR BUSINESS INTERRUPTION) HOWEVER CAUSED AND ON ANY
    THEORY OF LIABILITY, WHETHER IN CONTRACT, STRICT LIABILITY, OR TORT (INCLUDING NEGLIGENCE OR
    OTHERWISE) ARISING IN ANY WAY OUT OF THE USE OF THIS SOFTWARE, EVEN IF ADVISED OF THE
    POSSIBILITY OF SUCH DAMAGE.
*/

#include <Foundation/Foundation.h>
#include <loader.h>
#include <kurl.h>
#include <dom_doc.h>
#include <KWQKHTMLPart.h>
#include <WCURICache.h>

KHTMLPart::KHTMLPart(const KURL &url) {
    d = new KHTMLPartPrivate(this);
}

KHTMLPart::~KHTMLPart() {
    delete d;
    _logNotYetImplemented(); // FIXME
}

void KHTMLPart::slotData(id <WCURICacheData> data)  {
    if (!d->m_workingURL.isEmpty()) {
        begin(d->m_workingURL, 0, 0);
        d->m_workingURL = KURL();
    }
    write((const char *)[data cacheData], [data cacheDataSize]);
}

bool KHTMLPart::openURL(const KURL &url) {
    closeURL();
    d->m_workingURL = url;
    id <WCURICache> cache = WCGetDefaultURICache();
    NSString *nsurl = [NSString stringWithCString:url.url().latin1()];
    [cache requestWithString:nsurl requestor:d->m_recv userData:nil];
    return true;
}
```

computer to perform my job, I have to convert my C++ code into a computer-consumable binary form using a program called a *compiler*. This conversion process of human-readable to machine-runnable is called *compilation* or *building*. This translation procedure also explains why lines of code written in a programming language are called *source code*. They're the source material a compiler builds into (i.e., translates into) binary code the computer can execute.

Since full-featured programs like web browsers require so much source code—over 100,000 lines for a relatively succinct program like Konqueror—programmers break down all those lines into separate source code files. Doing this helps programmers organize and structure the separate subtasks. In the case of a web browser, the code for handling web addresses (URLs) might be contained in just one source code file, while a more sophisticated related area, like using URLs to download data from the internet, would be spread out over many source code files.

Chefs also break down their recipes into separate parts. For example, a recipe for Eggs Benedict would include a subrecipe for Hollandaise sauce, in addition to the instructions for poaching an egg, frying Canadian bacon, and toasting an English muffin. Yet a cookbook author might not copy a full description for Hollandaise sauce directly into the recipe for Eggs Benedict, especially if Hollandaise sauce is used elsewhere in the cookbook, perhaps in an asparagus preparation. A comprehensive cookbook would likely have only one Hollandaise sauce recipe and would refer to it everywhere else it's used: for example, "see Hollandaise sauce, p. 123."

Programmers do this too. When I'm writing

directive, which is akin to the cross-reference to Hollandaise sauce in the Eggs Benedict recipe. Include directives in software exist for the same reason as page cross-references in cookbooks. Such directives help programmers to stay organized and to have only one copy of a set of instructions for each specific task.

This system isn't perfect, since this cross-reference scheme introduces the possibility of mistakes. For example, if I'm in the middle of making a plate of Eggs Benedict and attempt to follow the cross-reference to Hollandaise sauce, but I turn to page 132 instead of 123 in my cookbook, I won't find what I'm looking for.

Mistakes like this happen all the time in programming. People are fallible and computers are unforgiving. Many things can go wrong when writing programs, like making an error in programming language syntax (akin to a spelling error in a cookbook) or referring to an incorrect file in an include directive (like looking on the wrong page for the Hollandaise sauce recipe). What's more, compilers don't have any capacity to understand what you mean if you don't say it exactly right.

Whenever I make an editing mistake in a program like the ones above, the compiler tells me about it with an *error message.* Compiler error messages are usually curt and precise: "expected expression, line 3, column 5." This unmet expectation could be a typo or a simple logic error, and the message telling me so is much like an executive chef in a busy kitchen who takes one look over the shoulder of a junior cook preparing a plate of Eggs Benedict and says, "Hollandaise too thick." Both messages are declarations of fault, and even if neither contains the exact remedial steps necessary to resolve the problem, both are genuinely useful.

When I cook, even when I follow an excellent cookbook recipe to the letter, the results can be mixed. Sometimes the finished food tastes good, sometimes it needs a bit more salt, and sometimes my kitchen skills let me down and the food doesn't turn out as well as I had hoped. On the computer, even after I fix all the compiler errors and get a program to build successfully, the program rarely does the desired job exactly right the first time. Code can compile successfully yet fail to produce the desired result, and innumerable behavior errors might occur in a complex program like a web browser: Text might be rendered in the wrong location, an image might be truncated due to a graphics bug, a button or link might not work when clicked. The program might also crash outright due to a serious programming error—akin to dropping a bowl of ingredients on the floor while cooking. Making fixes and improvements from the point after successful compilation but before achieving the intended software behavior is a matter of going back and trying again. Like trying to perfect a recipe in the kitchen, getting a program to build and run correctly takes a large number of tries—rewriting source code to improve the programming instructions, fixing compiler error messages, rebuilding the code, running the program or app, debugging, and then going back to the source code, to make edits and repeat the process over and over again, as you'll soon see.

* * *

Once we got our buy-in from management, Richard and I got together with Don in his office to hash out our porting strategy.

First, we had to go back to Richard's demo and finish uncutting the corners. To do that, we would copy the Konqueror source code files over to the Mac and get the code to build. After that, we could begin the testing and debugging process that would make the browser code seem like a natural part of the Mac software system.

Also, since Konqueror was free software, we had to comply with the Stallman-esque license the original authors had attached to it. Our management was willing to publish some software as open source, but it was keen to keep most code closed source and proprietary. The reason was simple. Mac OS X was a revenue producer for Apple. In the iPhone era, Apple took to publishing software updates for no charge, but back then, the company sold its Mac operating system in the United States for $129 per computer.[2] When we were developing our web browser strategy, the guidance from our executives was less a matter of "free as in freedom" or "free as in beer" and more "closed source as in money."

Don, Richard, and I had to work within this constraint, and as we hammered out the open versus closed aspect of our porting plan, an interesting dynamic began to play out among the three of us.

Don loved geeking out over the details of free software licenses. During his time at Netscape and Eazel, he had become knowledgeable on the topic, and he enjoyed going back and forth on the merits, drawbacks, and terms of different licenses. He took obvious pleasure in explaining the ramifications of the Lesser General Public License (LGPL), the free software license for the Konqueror source code. These terms stated that as long as we kept Konqueror in a separate chapter of the Mac cookbook, only used its code through cross-references, and freely published any alterations we made to Konqueror recipes to make them "taste good" on the Mac, we were in compliance with Stallman's free software license.

Richard didn't seem to care one whit about free software, and it wasn't beyond him to greet one of Don's long descriptions about software licenses with an eye roll or a sigh.

I was in the middle. I took free software licenses seriously. Respecting the conditions under which someone else made their work available was simply the right thing to do. What's more, if we hadn't honored Konqueror's license terms, we could have exposed Apple to legal action. I didn't want to obsess over licenses, but I thought it important to invest some time and careful thought to ensure we had the technical and legal bases covered.

Our different ways of approaching licenses made this software strategy session seem like a nerd reboot of "Goldilocks and the Three Bears." Fortunately, it wasn't too hard to get it "just right," and over a couple hours, we came up with our plan. To explain it, I'll turn once more to cookbooks.

Consider the many millions of lines of code that make up the Linux and Mac operating systems, and picture them as comprehensive cookbooks written by separate authors. There's overlap in the kind of recipes they offer, but the individual recipes themselves are different. The recipe book for the Mac didn't contain a web browser. The KDE section of the Linux cookbook had one, in a chapter titled "Konqueror." Our plan was to rip out this chapter, discard the remainder of the KDE and Linux volume, and add the Konqueror pages to the Mac cookbook. This would create an obvious problem. We would break every cross-reference Konqueror had to recipes in the parts of the cookbook we planned to throw away—there would be no Hollandaise recipe on p. 123.

To make this page-insertion scheme work, we would have to scrutinize each broken cross-reference in each Konqueror recipe as we brought it over to the Mac. When suitable equivalents already existed in Apple software—likely for common computing resources, such as colors or fonts—we could repoint the cross-reference to them. When equivalents didn't exist—say for a web page bookmarking system—we would need to write new recipes from scratch. We imagined that alterations would often be needed to recipes on both the Konqueror and Mac sides to make the "dishes" come out right.

In programming terms, once we copied the Konqueror code over to the Mac and tried to build it, we knew it wouldn't work right away—every broken cross-reference would result in a compiler error. We would have to fix all of these errors. After that, we wouldn't have a working browser right away. We knew there would be bugs in abundance. The point was that once we had the source code building, we would have the firm base of the Konqueror web browser to begin with, and from there, we could start debugging, testing, and polishing the code.

We added one final element to our strategy. We imagined that some parts of the Konqueror code would require an extra amount of programming attention before they would work well on the Mac. We decided to add annotations to the source code, reminders to ourselves to go back later to improve our adaptation of the code in that particular place. Programmers often use such notes. We call them "FIXMEs." For a big porting job like the one we were about to undertake, we expected to add a lot of FIXMEs. A couple months later, we would be very glad we had made this decision and that we had maintained the discipline to add these annotations whenever we had doubts about a piece of code while we were editing it. Each FIXME was another item on our programming to-do list.

Overall, our strategy had solid points in its favor. We were confident we could use Konqueror without running afoul of any free software license terms. Adding FIXMEs would lay the groundwork for the debugging after we got the software to build. The build phase, which would come first, would be straightforward—

across 300 source code files, and we estimated that getting every file to compile would take more than a month but less than two.

This sounded good at the time, but we simply weren't prepared for how tedious this build job would be. Here's how my days went during this phase of the project. I would try to build a Konqueror source code file, it would fail, and the compiler error message would tell me about a missing cross-reference, something that our page-tear-out scheme had broken. I would fix the problem and try to build again. Another error message. Another fix. And again. And again. It went on and on. Staring at the computer screen in my office. Building and reading and responding to compiler error messages. It began to feel like I was a character in an existentialist play, doomed to a repetitive colloquy with The Compiler:

ACT I. SCENE XXXVI.
Apple Infinite Loop Campus, Cupertino. Ken's office.

Ken is seated at his desk. His hands are on his keyboard. He types a command to invoke The Compiler on a file named kjs_binding.cpp.

THE COMPILER: kjs_binding.cpp: error on line 200:
    use of undeclared identifier "protocol"

Ken looks up the appropriate declaration for "protocol." He types it in.

KEN: Here you go, compiler. I've declared "protocol." Please try again.

Ken looks up the appropriate declaration for "host." He types it in.

KEN: Gosh, I'm sorry about that missing "host" identifier.
Here it is. Try now.

Once again, Ken types a command to invoke The Compiler on kjs_binding.cpp.

THE COMPILER: `kjs_binding.cpp: error on line 202: use of undeclared identifier "port"`

Don and Richard endured this build ordeal along with me, and during lunch and coffee breaks we commiserated with each other about how bored we were. We couldn't fob this work off on junior programmers or interns either. Apple didn't work like that. Secrecy was one reason, but, more important, Apple didn't separate research and development from software implementation. We were responsible for coming up with the ideas for our web browser and writing the shipping code that went out to customers too.

There was no exit from the tedium. We just had to keep going. Yet, every hour of monotony was a contribution to our porting strategy, and every file we went through was an opportunity to read and learn about our adopted source code. Slowly, day after day, week after week, we whittled down the list of files we still needed to build.

Our estimate of two months was about right. We finally got to the end of the compiler error messages. Konqueror built on the Mac, and we had a double-clickable app. When we launched it, our new browser app displayed an empty white window. Now we had to get our code to do what browser apps exist to do: load web pages. It couldn't yet, and many times our app crashed when we tried. Other times the browser didn't appear to do anything at all.

This is where our idea of adding FIXMEs paid dividends. We wrote code to autogenerate a report as we attempted to load a web page. Every FIXME in our code added an entry to this report, which made it clear that, behind the scenes, in the depths of our software, our browser was doing a lot, even if it didn't yet produce visible web pages.

The three of us took to positioning a FIXME reporting window next to the browser app window on our screens, and we would closely eye the report as we tried out our browser. The workflow became: Try to load a page, inspect the report, change the source code to patch up the most glaring problem the FIXMEs seemed to show, then try again.

At the very start of this debugging phase, this report contained entries like: "Rendering images not implemented . . . Web page links not implemented . . . Running JavaScript code not implemented." Later on, as we made improvements to the code, we updated many of these "not implemented" entries to "partially implemented," and when we felt an area with a FIXME was finally in good shape, we removed the annotation altogether. And yet, after fixing scores of these problems, our browser window showed no signs of responding whatsoever. It remained an empty expanse of white pixels while the voluminous FIXME report continued to point out how much we had left to do.

We kept going, and after more weeks of tedious work, Richard had to take a couple of days off. He had been focusing on the graphics routines essential to rendering elements on the screen. He believed he was close to eliminating the need for a few critical FIXMEs. He briefed me, and I picked up the work where he left off. After a few hours of analysis, I found a place where it seemed like the software was, in anthropomorphic terms, going through the motions of drawing a web page without actually putting the pen down on the page. It was like a web browser version of air guitar. I wrote some code to address this, then I built the browser app and launched it.

I typed in a URL: http://www.yahoo.com. The FIXME report filled up with line after line as it always did, but the browser didn't crash. A few seconds passed, and then the browser did something. It drew me a picture.

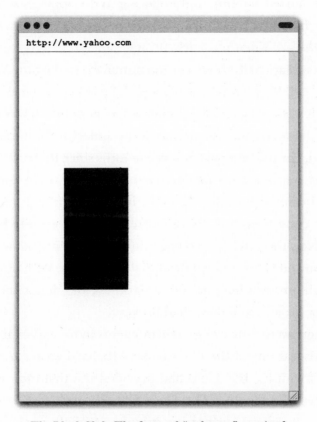

The Black Slab. The first real "web page" our Apple browser ever loaded from the internet.

I quit the browser app and tried again. I loaded the Yahoo! home page just like before. The FIXME report filled up, the browser didn't crash, I got the same brief pause . . . then the same black rectangle.

I ran down the hall to get Don. When we got back, I quit the browser and loaded the Yahoo! main page again. We held our breath through the same pause . . . and we then saw the same black rectangle. The browser had finally done something!

We started hooting and hollering and clapping each other on the back. We acted like we were in the scene from *2001: A Space Odyssey*, when our early primate ancestors were visited by the alien Black Slab about a dozen minutes into the film. Well, we aped them. We pointed and whooped. I tried the page load once more. It worked again . . . another black monolith! It was real!

While this achievement may seem underwhelming, we were thrilled. For the best part of three months since Richard's demo, we had put our faith in our porting strategy, even though it yielded results we could track only indirectly through numbers: source code files built, cross-references fixed up, FIXMEs retired. Now we could *see* web pages in the browser window.

Don and I had our own Black Slab Encounter. We had slogged through our own long period of darkness and doubt about our browser project, and dawn had broken.

There were only two *Eureka!* moments in my career at Apple, and this was one of them. I was sorry Richard wasn't around to share it with us. His demo had provided the first indication of Konqueror's potential. The Black Slab Encounter was the next big step. It showed our porting strategy was really working, making it a milestone in our effort to turn our demo into a product.

We would never again endure a period where we went weeks without visible evidence of progress. Once we started to see web pages loading, we could also see our browser getting better, almost on a daily basis. Before the week was out, we turned the black rectangle into a page displaying all the text on the Yahoo! home page. A couple days after that, web links were rendering with the blue underline style then prevalent. The following week, the first images appeared. When I loaded that first web page, it was like I had thrown a switch, and the lights finally came on.

These days, most of us take web browsers for granted, so the analogy to lights is apt. We surf the web all the time without thinking about browsers as a technology that had to be created. The same goes for electric lighting, and I think we can learn something about our twenty-first-century efforts with our browser by looking closer at Edison's nineteenth-century approach to inventing his lightbulb.

Edison too had his technical struggles, including his search for a lightbulb filament material that would burn brightly and last long. I enjoy this quaint description of his quest, which comes from a 1910 book titled *The Story of Great Inventions*:

[Edison] sat one night thinking about the problem, unconsciously fingering a bit of lampblack [a pigment made from soot] mixed with tar which he had used in his telephone. Not thinking what he was doing, he rolled this mixture of tar and lampblack into a thread. Then he noticed what he had done, and the thought occurred to him: "Why not pass an electric current though this carbon?" He tried it. A faint glow was the result . . .

He next set out to find the best kind of carbon for the purpose. He carbonized paper and wood of various kinds—in fact, everything he could find that would yield a carbon filament. He tried the fibers of a Japanese fan made of bamboo, and found that this gave a better light than anything he had tried before. He then began the search for the best kind of bamboo. He learned that there are about twelve hundred varieties of bamboo. He must have a sample of every variety. He sent men to every part of the world where bamboo grows. One man travelled thirty thousand miles and had many encounters with wild beasts in his search for bamboo. At last, a Japanese bamboo was found that was better than any other. The search for the carbon fiber had cost about a hundred thousand dollars.[3]

This little story has it all: Flashes of inspiration! Intrepid men! Vast distances! Wild beasts! Huge sums of money! Even the author of *The Story of Great Inventions* has a suitably tall-tale-telling name, Elmer Ellsworth Burns.

Of course, the real lightbulb development story is more complicated, and I think we might reasonably question whether Edison really did absentmindedly finger lampblack and tar and then come up with the gee-whiz thought of passing an electric current through the wirelike result. As Steven Johnson says in his book, *Where Good Ideas Come From*, "Folklore calls Edison the inventor of the lightbulb, but in truth the lightbulb came into being through a complex network of interaction between Edison and his rivals . . . Edison built on the designs of at least a half dozen other inventors who went before him, including Joseph Swan and William Sawyer."[4]

Edison didn't dream up the idea of electric lighting on his own, and carbon had been used in lightbulb filament investigations long before Edison started looking into its suitability—Joseph Swan experimented with carbon extensively. Yet such predecessors failed to create a practical lightbulb. Edison succeeded. Why? An adequate explanation must include Edison's conception of electric lighting as a complex electric generation and distribution system, his already-established track record as an inventor, his ability to parlay his reputation into the necessary corporate funding for his investigations, and his vision to establish and lead one of the first product-oriented research and development labs, an organization that efficiently coordinated the efforts of many.[5]

All this mattered, but I think Edison's large-scale success was built on a foundation of tending to small details. I would like to turn the discussion back to how Edison himself described his approach for constructing the foundations for his innovative work, specifically, how he solved problems like finding the best filament material for his lightbulb: "None of my inventions came by accident. I see a worthwhile need to be met and I make trial after trial until it comes. What it boils down to is one per cent inspiration and ninety-nine per cent perspiration."[6]

In saying this, has Edison himself engaged in his own Burnsian oversimplification? If Edison really wanted to spin a compelling self-serving myth about his powers as an inventor, he might have come up with a better explanation than saying, essentially, "I worked hard." As myth, this rates poorly. It's unmysterious. It's as if Edison is telling us that, even if the twirling of tar and lampblack had happened exactly as Burns described it, such bursts of insight don't matter that much in the big picture. For Edison, it was more important to build on promising ideas and keep working and working until an invention was made real.

As an engineer, I'm interested in Edison's concrete numbers. This 1:99 relationship of inspiration to perspiration sounds like a lot. Is it? The story of our Apple web browser development provides some data to check. Richard's demo served as our inspiration. Don, Richard, and I proceeded together from there, and we worked hard up until the Black Slab Encounter. Here's a rough breakdown of the hours.

BROWSER PROJECT EDISON RATIO

INSPIRATION

FLASH OF INSIGHT TO GET FROM NOTHING TO RICHARD'S DEMO

1	×	8	×	2	×	1	=	16
ENGINEER		HOURS/DAY		DAYS		WEEK		HOURS

PERSPIRATION

HARD WORK TO GET FROM RICHARD'S DEMO TO BLACK SLAB ENCOUNTER

3	×	8	×	5	×	10	=	1200
ENGINEERS		HOURS/DAY		DAYS/WEEK		WEEKS		HOURS

INSPIRATION : PERSPIRATION = **1:75**

RATIO

At first glance, this ratio of 1:75 shows that Edison may have overestimated the amount of required effort by around 25 percent, and that would be a significant error. However, in making his full 1:99 claim, Edison was talking about *finished* inventions. As I said, the Black Slab Encounter was an important milestone for us on the browser project, but we were still a year away from being done. Remember what the Black Slab indicated—it was the first time our new browser code did anything, other than failing to respond, crashing, or amassing FIXME reports. And yet, even though we were still at such an early stage in the overall development of our program, with many months ahead of us before we could consider ourselves to have produced a finished product, we were already at seventy-five parts perspiration to one part inspiration. From this perspective, Edison grossly underestimated.

I doubt Edison believed he was proposing a physical law or had any expectations his 1:99 ratio was a universal constant. Even so, his experience taught him something about producing inventions: Hard work was essential. And yet, looking back to the Burns excerpt, twirling the tar and lampblack has equal stature in the narrative as the worldwide search for the best filament material. If Edison's 1:99 ratio is to be believed, then Burns greatly inflates the role of inspiration in his account, and perhaps that's why Edison spoke up for the necessary investment of effort to go from an idea to an invention.

We want to believe geniuses like Edison can conjure world-changing inventions out of thin air. Easy explanations are alluring, and Edison-like inspiration seems magical. Perspiration, we know, involves drudgery. When Burns crafted his popular retellings of famous inventions like the incandescent lightbulb, he highlighted an imagined magical moment. Edison knew the actual story was more about the drudgery.

I agree with Edison. Ideas are nothing without the hard work to make them real. So it was for Edison in his search to find the best lightbulb filament material, and although our results with our web browser certainly were less profound for humanity, so it was for us.

Consider where we would have been weeks after Richard's demo if we hadn't developed our porting strategy and set about executing it. We would have been no better off than Don and I were after our initial six weeks of investigation leading up to Richard's arrival at Apple. We would have been nowhere with nothing to show. Richard's demo would have been little more than a programming curiosity if the three of us hadn't gritted our teeth, kept our noses to the grindstone, and thrown all the hard-work maxims we could think of into building the code, fixing cross-references one at a time, studying FIXMEs, and producing the Black Slab Encounter.

But was that it? Was making a web browser just a matter of a good demo plus some programming elbow grease? And what about that elbow grease? Since Edison suggests that dreaming and brainstorming consume so little time, then what is this 99 percent of toil that takes up the remainder?

In deceptively brief terms, Edison tells us: "I make trial after trial until it comes." He and his team were willing to perspire, but he also knew what he would be doing with all those hours: trial and error. For the lightbulb, filaments were the key, and bamboo was the most promising material, so Edison tested every kind of bamboo to find the best. If Burns is to be believed, there were twelve hundred varieties of bamboo, and Edison tried each one. It sounds simple, and it was, but the way Edison defined the project also gave it a shape. He crossed off items from a to-do list.

When we made our porting strategy for the web browser, we turned to something like Edison's model. We knew the compiler would tell us about broken cross-references, and we examined all of them one at a time. We knew our FIXMEs would tell us where out code was weakest, and we studied the reports closely. Moving toward the Black Slab Encounter was a stepwise process, much like Edison's search for the best bamboo. Edison did trial after trial with filaments; we went file after file in our build process and FIXME after FIXME trying to load a web page. Both projects were built on unglamorous grunt work, but the specifics matter. Edison wasn't just trudging toward the horizon in a desert, hoping that the crest of the next sand dune would reveal an oasis—that sounds more like the way that Don and I wandered through our browser investigations in the weeks before Richard joined us. Instead, Edison searched specifically for the best kind of bamboo, and he was undaunted by the need to check a vast number of varieties. Each one he tested was an item crossed off and brought him closer to finding which one was the best. In the lead up to the Black Slab Encounter, we did the same. Even though Don, Richard, and I struggled with the tedium, we kept plowing through each file and FIXME.

Hard work is hard. Inspiration does not pay off without diligence. We collaborated to get through the drudgery. Our knowledge of our craft—code, compilers, software licenses, and debugging—gave us the confidence to forge ahead and to invest and direct the necessary time and effort to make Richard's demo pay off.

Of course, a program that produced nothing but a Black Slab was far from a fully functioning web browser. We were still a long way from delivering a finished app, but our technical dawn had broken, the lights were now on, so at least we could see where we were going.

4

One Simple Rule

We'd begun as three programmers trying to kick-start a project. Within a few months, we'd hired a few more people, and we were nine, a small web browser software team starting to hit its stride.

By that time, word had come down the management chain. Steve Jobs himself had decided how he would judge our browser as a product. The focus would be on one thing: speed. Steve wanted our browser to be fast, really fast at loading web pages from the internet, much faster than Microsoft Internet Explorer, the default browser on the Mac, the product we aimed to replace.

At Apple, we always tried to deliver the best product out of the box, and in addition to this speed directive, we needed to deliver a browser with a well-rounded set of features—excellent bookmark management and a streamlined user interface were high on the list. Yet the team jelled around our speed goal. The challenge gave us a purpose. Our chat channel, which ran on an Internet Relay Chat (IRC) server, buzzed with technical questions, comments on the latest problem, ideas for solving them, proposals for code changes. At least four or five of us ate lunch together every day, and we would walk down to Caffè Macs in a little posse, crossing the Cupertino campus green space from Infinite Loop 2 to Infinite Loop 4 in a tight group so we could all share in whatever geeky conversation we were having. I started a tradition of waiting at the lunch table for everyone to arrive with their cafeteria selection before I started eating, and I good-naturedly shamed everyone into doing the same—wordlessly, with a sideways stare, a lowered chin, and a raised brow. We took our first bites together. We weren't a family, but we were a close-knit team. We were a model of Apple-style collaboration, a small group focused on a shared objective, and ours was developing a fast web browser.

In addition, we were keenly aware that product replacements like the one we were attempting could be a delicate business. Once Apple made our new browser the default on the Mac, none of us wanted our users to question whether we had given them an improved web surfing experience. Steve reasoned that a speedy new Apple browser would be the best way to make people forget about Internet Explorer and to feel good about our replacement right away.

Speed was also part of Steve's vision for the future of internet connectivity. It can be painful to recall the glacial pace of surfing the web in the early 2000s if you lived through it, when hardly anyone had what we would now consider "broadband." Web pages often jumped around as they loaded; many images came through in a few blurry stages before sharpening up. Everyone knew faster days were coming, and Steve wanted our browser to be ready right away for the increased data that would be flowing through internet connections as they got quicker. Our code had to keep up. Steve thought speed was the long-term key to better browsing, so making a high-performance browser became our top priority, our definition for greatness.

We still had a long way to go. By the late spring of 2002, our web browser was still only capable of crawling. We couldn't use it for our daily browsing—or anything close. Sometimes the text of articles on news sites would be an illegible jumble; shopping carts on commerce sites would lose track of items; login forms for banking sites would fail, preventing us from checking our account balances. Not to mention that our browser was *slow*: slow to load data from the internet, slow to draw images, slow to go back to the previous page.

Fixing the bugs that prevented websites from looking and working correctly took up much of our time, but given our Steve-mandated speed directive, we also had to figure how to make the browser run faster.

Don was the one who figured out how we would make our code quick. One day, a month or two after the Black Slab Encounter, he called me into his office and asked me to create a test program to measure browser speed. He envisioned an automated tool that would launch our browser app and command it to load a suite of web pages, one after the other, in rapid succession. Over the next couple days, I wrote the code to do just that. I named it the Page Load Test, but we soon took to calling the PLT.

The PLT became our software conditioning coach, one with the demeanor of a drill sergeant holding a virtual stopwatch. When we clicked the Start button in the PLT window, the test program looked at the first URL on its list, metaphorically hollered this web address at the browser, clicked its stopwatch, and waited, tapping its toe, as the browser loaded the page. Once the page was completely loaded and rendered, the PLT clicked its stopwatch again, noted the time on its clipboard, and then shouted the next address on the list.

Don chose each of the forty web pages in the PLT suite to make the trial for our code as punishing as possible. He selected pages heavy on text, like Yahoo!, and others packed with graphics, like Disney. His list pointed to some of the most visited destinations on the web. Some, like Amazon, Google, and eBay, you'll recognize. Others are nearly forgotten, like Real Networks, Webcrawler, and iVillage. Together, they covered every important attribute of web page loading and rendering, to expose any weakness in our browser.

After the PLT got to the end of its URL list, it would calculate the average time to load a web page. This was a distilled-down measure for how fast our browser was at that moment, and this single number became the key element to Don's plan. He issued a managerial edict: No more code changes without running the PLT.

What does this PLT pronouncement mean, and why was it important? On our browser team, as in most serious software development efforts, we followed an editorial process to make changes to our source code. Whenever I finished editing some code, I would write a detailed summary of what my edits did, what feature it implemented or what bug it fixed, and how well I thought my code change accomplished these goals. Then I would find a teammate to review the work with me. The code review process often led to round after round of reviewer feedback, improvements, and requests for re-review. Once everything passed muster in the peer review, and only then, was I allowed to commit my change to our repository, the central server that stored all the revisions to all our source code.

Before the PLT, our editorial process was primarily concerned with feature implementation, bug fixes, and web standards compliance—how well the browser did what it was supposed to do.

These were all qualitative measures. The PLT checked for speed, a quantitative test, and it introduced an independent evaluation to every code change we made. Correctness and speed now went hand in hand. Don held that if we heeded the PLT without fail and rejected any code changes that made our code slower, only two things could happen. Either the browser would stay the same speed . . . or it would get faster. He would tap his index finger to his temple to punctuate his explanation of this sneaky logic. From the day the PLT was finished, Don declared, our browser would become faster by never getting slower. It was his Zen koan.

Running the PLT against new code became a daily ritual, sometimes an hourly one. I often used it to test which of two equivalent but subtly different pieces of code was faster. When it came time to make a code change, everything was fine if the browser ran as fast with the new code in place as it did without it. Most code edits had no effect on performance, but some inevitably did, and as long as the change was in the faster direction, then all was well. We sometimes had happy accidents too—unforeseen speedups stemming from changes to remove lingering FIXMEs. Higher-quality code often performs faster.

As we untangled those columns of text from news sites, and fixed e-commerce shopping carts so they always remembered your items, and improved compatibility with banking sites so you could manage your money online, we had to change the code to make these features and functions perform correctly while avoiding making the browser any slower.

There could be no exceptions to the PLT speed rule—Don wouldn't allow it. When an essential bit of new code caused a slowdown, things could get tricky. Finding remedies for speed setbacks typically involved the prickly issue of software optimization, and that term warrants some explanation.

* * *

There aren't many famous computer scientists, even among programmers, but Donald Knuth is rightly revered. He is the author of *The Art of Computer Programming*, one of the foundational texts of computer science, a multivolume treatise that he's been writing, with something approximating monklike asceticism and devotion, since 1962.[1] Knuth undertakes meticulous research, writes with extreme care, and issues publications with titles like *Introduction to Combinatorial Algorithms and Boolean Functions, Bitwise Tricks & Techniques; Binary Decision Diagrams*, and *Generating All Trees—History of Combinatorial Generation*. For software developers who take their work seriously, Knuth is the consummate craftsman. Here's what he has to say about optimization:

> Programmers waste enormous amounts of time thinking about, or worrying about, the speed of noncritical parts of their programs, and these attempts at efficiency actually have a strong negative impact when debugging and maintenance are considered. We should forget about small efficiencies, say about 97% of the time: *premature optimization is the root of all evil.*[2] (Emphasis added.)

Optimization is the process where programmers try to make code execute faster. Isn't that what the PLT was all about? So, isn't optimization a good thing? Not always, and if the Knuthian numerical estimate is to be given the credence it deserves, and he is an extraordinarily deliberative man, then optimization is bad about 97 percent of the time. Why?

Programs are, after all, just long lists of instructions for computers, and although computers are very fast, they are not infinitely so. To make speedy software, program instructions must be as efficient as possible, but it's not always straightforward to know which instructions will be fast to execute.

Here's an example. If I invited you over to the kitchen in my home for the purpose of a demonstration, and I asked you to:

- Take a jar of mustard out of my refrigerator.

you would accomplish this task easily, since my kitchen is well stocked with condiments. It's also clear this instruction would take less time to perform than this instruction of similar length:

- Go to the supermarket to buy a jar of mustard.

Since some instructions encapsulate a higher order of conceptual complexity than others, some instructions take longer, perhaps much longer, to execute than others. If I remained in my kitchen while we conducted this mustard jar performance test, I could probably take out and return the jar from my refrigerator many dozens of times before you could bring one back from the store. But then again, that would depend on how close we were to the supermarket. For the purpose of understanding optimization better, the key word in the previous sentence is *depend.* Sophisticated software is built on an elaborate and interlocking web of dependencies between separate components, and dealing with these relationships is an inescapable part of writing complicated software like a web browser. The mustard jar example begins to illustrate how basic this problem is, hints at how deep it goes, and shows how difficult it can be for a programmer to know how fast a specific piece of code might execute just by looking at it, even if the content of the instruction is perfectly easy to understand.

How does this relate to optimization? Here's a set of instructions to accomplish another kitchen task:

- Take everything out of my refrigerator.
- Put all the items on the counter.

And an attempt to optimize it:

- Take everything out of my refrigerator.
- Put all the items on the counter.
- Use as few armloads as possible.

This third instruction makes a suggestion about the speed of executing this task. The number of trips between refrigerator and counter is posited as the logjam, and the implication is that if the number of go-rounds could be reduced, then the overall operation could be accomplished faster.

Is that right? This optimization attempt raises several questions. Loading and unloading a few big armloads of stuff might actually be faster . . . but is it really? If I try to assemble and juggle a large armload of mustard and mayonnaise jars and milk cartons and sticks of butter and that plastic container of pork stir-fry leftovers from last night, what if I drop something in the effort to carry all these items at once? That's a bug, right? If I spill or break something, do I have to take time to clean up the mess before the task is considered done? If I go back to the "Use as few armloads as possible" directive to think more about what it means, I still come away thinking the goal is to minimize the number of trips between fridge and counter—but is that the actual reason? I don't know. It's simply my best guess. I don't have enough context about the underlying goal of the task to be absolutely sure.

This scenario shows why an experienced programmer like Knuth thought to issue an admonition against optimizations. The additional "Use as few armloads as possible" instruction causes an increased potential for bugs, introduces ambiguity that makes the code more difficult to change down the line, since we don't really know the core reasoning behind the step, and the end result might not even be faster. This tacked-on "optimization" instruction might be causing a lot more trouble than it was worth. Knuth suggested that 97 percent of the time, it was.

This gets to the heart of why the PLT was such an important test. The PLT helped us to understand what our programming instructions were doing along the essential axis of speed and showed us precisely when and where we were introducing slowness to our source code. The PLT told us when to pay attention to the "small efficiencies" Knuth mentioned. It was our 3 percent escape hatch, a way to know for sure that optimization wasn't "premature." We were sure each optimization we did was helping to keep performance heading in the right direction.

There's a conventional view in software engineering that the "prematurity" Knuth mentioned has something to do with a project's schedule. It's common for programming teams to make their code work correctly first and then turn to speeding it up only once most of the bugs are fixed. Front-loading feature work and back-loading performance optimizations are typical. Yet, when features take longer to complete than expected and the delivery schedule can't be shifted, management might have no choice but to drop performance work entirely.

Since we had our performance directive from Steve, we couldn't let this happen, and Don figured out how to prevent it. He had us carefully choose our optimization opportunities based on clear and provable knowledge about what was slow and hash things out right at the moment we found the slowness. The PLT helped us to correctly distribute optimization work throughout the entire project. We optimized when we knew what we were doing, in direct response to measuring code with the PLT.

Yet, even with the PLT, optimizing remained a tricky business, and sometimes the search for performance improvements led to detailed investigations on why things work the way they do and how they might work differently. For example, optimizing that refrigerator-emptying task in my kitchen example might require a comprehensive investigation to determine the largest set of items a person could carry in a single armload with the least chance of dropping any. It might involve thinking through the off-loading procedure to find the best way to position items on the counter. Finding the fastest method might come down to sideways thinking—if minimizing fridge-counter round trips is really best, then it might be a good idea to invest the time to fetch a box from a closet or from the garage so all the refrigerator items could be carried at once, rather than using several armloads.

Sometimes, in the development of the browser, even our best investigations and "thinking outside the box" ideas weren't sufficient. There were plenty of instances when we were about to integrate a new feature, only to find that there truly was no way to add the code without a negative impact on speed. As we introduced features like clicking the back button to return you to your previously viewed web page, we found we couldn't perform the bookkeeping to maintain the previous page at quick readiness without impeding the load of all pages. The PLT showed the slowdown. When we deemed such features too important to skip but couldn't figure out how to add them without causing such slowdowns, we instituted a trading scheme, where we found speedups in unrelated parts of our existing source code to "pay for" the performance cost of the new features. When we looked around for code to perform this kind of payoff optimization, we typically targeted code we knew well and that was stable, preferably both. Once found, we tuned this proxy code to function the same, only faster, and sufficiently faster that we wound up with either a nil or a positive net impact on performance when we added both the feature-laden code and the speed-payoff code to our project.

None of this optimization was easy, and it wasn't always fun, but Don always held the line. And in the year following the Black Slab Encounter, we succeeded in making our code faster and faster.

As we got close to the release date for our project, Apple's marketing department set out to pick an official name for our browser. Within a month before the worldwide announcement of our app, planned for Macworld Expo SF in early 2003, we were still calling it either WebBrowser or Alexander, the latter a code name evoking the great Macedonian king, a famous "Konqueror." We thought this was clever, but it wouldn't work as a customer-facing name for an Apple product. Scott Forstall and the marketing department asked the browser team for our name ideas, but I was so focused on getting the browser code done that I made only halfhearted suggestions, and now I can't remember what they were.

Steve Jobs had some name ideas, and when I first heard them, I cringed. Early on, Steve liked "Thunder," but he soon got over that in favor of "Freedom." I thought both were awful names. I just couldn't imagine telling people, "I work on Freedom," as if I were some semidelusional comic book superhero wannabe.

It was Scott who ultimately came up with the name that stuck: Safari. It conveyed the same world-traveler feel as other well-known browsers—Navigator, Explorer, Konqueror—but it wasn't a slavish knock-off. It was fresh. Don liked it too and, more important, so did Steve.

Also around this time, I also got the confirmation our developer toolkit would be called WebKit, a name I had tentatively scribbled on the whiteboard in the very first porting strategy meeting I had with Don and Richard many months earlier.

Safari would be my first Apple product release, thrilling enough by itself, and then Don told me that the potential for thrills was ratcheting up. He would be attending the final rehearsals for the Steve Jobs keynote at Moscone Center in San Francisco and he invited me to join him. It wasn't a vacation; we'd be there to troubleshoot.

Don's seat-of-the-pants plan was that if Steve ran into some glitch during the Safari demo rehearsal, he would be there to say "Yes sir, Steve, we'll get everything fixed up right away," and then he and I would figure out what was wrong, as The Man, a supremely restless audience, watched and waited.

In later years, I would learn more about how Steve prepared for these big-splash product announcements. Three weeks or a month before the keynote itself, Steve would start rehearsing with portions of his slide deck in some venue at Apple, often in Town Hall, the auditorium on the Infinite Loop campus. Slowly, day by day, he would build the show by stepping through it as he wanted to present it at the keynote. This was one of Steve's great secrets of success as a presenter. He practiced. A lot. He went over and over the material until he had the presentation honed, and he knew it cold.

Up on stage in Moscone, Steve rehearsed in a way that was new to me, and once I saw his technique, it seemed so right to me that I've used it myself for my own presentation rehearsals ever since. When Steve spoke to a slide, he went fully into his keynote persona. His tone of voice, his stance, his gestures, everything was exactly as if he were presenting to a packed house. For as long as everything proceeded to his satisfaction, he kept going. As needed, he stopped, stepped out of character, reduced the volume of his voice, and asked executives seated in the front row, like Phil Schiller, the company's senior vice president of Worldwide Marketing, what they thought of some turn of phrase or whether they believed ideas flowed together smoothly. Feedback received, Steve would pause quite deliberately for a second or two, go back into character, and resume his keynote persona. If a phrase still didn't run right, he would pause, back up, and try again. Sometimes he did this three or four times, each time with an absolutely clear separation between attempts, like takes on a movie set. He never truly bungled a line—his presentation was already polished by this point—but he was committed to making every slide and every phrase better if he could.

Steve ran through his entire presentation, from start to finish, twice each on the Saturday and Sunday preceding the keynote itself, which was planned for Tuesday, January 7, 2003. These were actual dress rehearsals. I could tell. Steve wore a black mock turtleneck and jeans.

Steve started this keynote with a company update that highlighted the Switcher campaign, Apple's then-popular marketing effort designed at getting people to buy a Mac to replace their Windows computers. In this pre-iPod/iPhone/iPad era, Apple, Inc. was still Apple Computer, a PC company trying to drum up customers to raise its single-digit market share. Part of the strategy to increase sales had been the opening, two years earlier, of the first Apple Stores, retail locations that aimed to provide better customer service and an improved buying experience for Macs. Industry prognosticators had scorned the Apple retail effort when it began in 2001, and even old Apple executives like the former chief financial officer, Joseph Graziano, suggested, "Apple's problem is it still believes the way to grow is serving caviar in a world that seems pretty content with cheese and crackers."[3] Now, almost two years after the first store opened, Steve was ready to declare that there was quite an appetite for caviar. To back up the retail success story with hard numbers, he shared a report of $148 million in Apple Store revenues in the preceding holiday quarter.[4]

With that done, Steve was ready to wrap up this initial section of his presentation, and he said, "That's the update on Apple retail stores. We could not be happier, and I hope that we've won over some of the critics who, when we opened our first stores, said we would most certainly fail."

By this point in Sunday morning's rehearsal, everyone in the hall, a few dozen of us, expected Steve to pause for dramatic effect, draw a breath, and then proceed directly to the next section of the show, a computers-in-education initiative, just as he had done twice the previous day.

Instead, Steve said, "Actually, here's what I have to say to those people who said our stores would most certainly fail," and he clicked to a newly inserted slide.

He played it perfectly straight, and his punch line killed. After a moment of stunned silence, the room rocked with laughter. Steve had to take five while everyone caught hold of themselves. It's well known that Steve could be feisty, but he could also be genuinely funny.

Of course, two days later, during the real keynote, he didn't show his humorously testy slide, and it was the Safari section of the keynote that mattered to us anyway. I still remember the clammy-hand feeling as Steve did the reveal: Apple had made its own web browser. In a flash, our super-secret, eighteen-month-long project became public knowledge. Steve also announced that Safari not only loaded web pages faster than Internet Explorer . . . it loaded web pages *three times faster.*

After Steve showed the Safari icon, he clicked to the next slide. It had a single word: Why? Steve felt the need to say why Apple had made its own browser, and his explanation led with speed. Some may have thought that touting Safari performance was just marketing, a retrospective cherry-picking of one browser attribute that just happened to turn out well.

I knew better. I had been part of the team that had received the speed mandate months earlier, and I had participated in the actions he now described which ensured the speed of our browser.

Such connections of words to actions can be meaningful, and in our case they were, since the words led to the actions we used to make our product. This clear connection of words to actions in a product development cycle was new to me. We certainly never had anything like it at Eazel, my former company, and it made me wonder if this experience on Safari was a fluke.

When I looked outside software for examples to test my fluke-or-not hypothesis, sports was an obvious candidate. Since games in major sports happen much more often than Apple announces products, there are many more opportunities to check the connection between words and actions. Coaches and players are also more forthcoming when speaking to the media, since teams rarely impose Apple-style secrecy. Combined with the win-or-lose nature of sports, we might hope for a link between the quality of discourse and the likelihood of victory.

Usually this disappoints. When a baseball reporter asks a pitcher to comment on his just-completed winning performance in a postgame, locker-room interview, the response is typically content-free patter: "Well, Bob, my curveball was working great tonight, and right now, I'm just taking it one game at a time."[5]

Such comments explain little and predict nothing.

Yet words and actions can connect in sports, and when they do, as in football, in the head coaching career of Vince Lombardi, the link becomes illuminating and Apple-like.

When Lombardi joined the Green Bay Packers in 1959, the team had gone eleven straight seasons without a winning record, and after winning only one of twelve games the previous year, the team fired Lombardi's predecessor.

Upon arriving at training camp as their new head coach, Lombardi made an immediate and indelible first impression on Bart Starr, a struggling third-string, fourth-year quarterback.

After leading the players to a meeting room, Lombardi waited in front of a portable blackboard as the players sat down. He picked up a piece of chalk and began to speak.

> "Gentlemen," he said, "we have a great deal of ground to cover. We're going to do things a lot differently than they've been done here before . . . [We're] going to relentlessly chase perfection, knowing full well we will not catch it, because perfection is not attainable. But we are going to relentlessly chase it because, in the process, we will catch excellence."[6]

He paused and stared, his eyes moving from player to player. The room was silent. "I'm not remotely interested in being just good," he said with an intensity that startled them all.

During a break in the meeting, Starr bolted for the phone to call his wife in Alabama. "Honey, we're going to start to win. The guy talked about perfection!"[7]

Of course, any coach can hold a miniature pep rally, but Lombardi soon followed up on his rah-rah cheer with a clear-cut description of the specific thing they would perfect. One play. One single running play. Lombardi told his assembled players: "Gentlemen, this is the most important play we have. It's the play we must make go. It's the play that we *will* make go. It's the play that we will run again, and again, and again."[8]

Lombardi describes this play in detail in *The Science and Art of Football.*[9] This charming, low-budget, sixties-style instructional film opens with clips of game footage set to martial music and then cuts to a studio shot of Lombardi, gap-toothed, bespectacled, white shirt and dark tie, close-cropped hair, and holding a football in front of him so he won't be mistaken for an insurance salesman, as he introduces, a bit haltingly in his Brooklyn accent, the focus of his intense quest for perfection: the Power Sweep.

In the movie, Lombardi talks for the best part of a half hour about this one play, pointer in hand, motioning at a blackboard full of X's and O's as he details the concepts, the assignments, the options, and the coaching points of this bare-knuckles tactic, where the quarterback hands the ball off to a running back, who then takes several strides parallel to the line of scrimmage before picking up blocks and turning upfield to grind out yardage and march his team toward the opponent's goal line. A few minutes into his filmed lecture detailing his favorite offensive play, Lombardi is overcome by his enthusiasm for the Power Sweep. He forgets his awkwardness in front of the camera and assumes the hunkered-down stance of an offensive lineman to demonstrate the proper blocking technique with whole-body gesticulation.

You wouldn't think that there was so much to say about a single running play, but perhaps *The Science and Art of Football* was edited for length. Famous coach and broadcaster John Madden described attending a coaching clinic where Lombardi talked about the Power Sweep, and only the Power Sweep, *for eight hours*.[10]

Through practice after practice, drill after drill, game after game, and season after season, the Packers honed and refined Lombardi's Power Sweep. Even though opposing teams knew the play was coming, they couldn't stop it. In a seeming attempt to disprove Sun Tzu's dictum that "all warfare is based on deception," Lombardi built his victories on an openly declared challenge. To beat the Packers, you must beat the Power Sweep.

In Lombardi's first year, with essentially the same players as the year before, the Packets won seven and lost five. The year after that, they went to the NFL championship game, but lost. Over the following seven years, the Packers won five championships, including victories in the first two Super Bowls, a step-by-step, year-by-year progression through the ranks from worst to best to legends, all built on the foundations of one humble running play, initially described on the blackboard and then executed exquisitely on the field over and over again.

In any complex effort, communicating a well-articulated vision for what you're trying to do is the starting point for figuring out how to do it. And though coming up with such a vision is difficult, it's unquestionably more difficult to complete the entire circuit, to come up with an idea, a plan to realize the idea, and then actualize the plan at a high standard, all without getting bogged down, changing direction entirely, or failing outright. Perhaps the most unnerving and fear-inducing source of anxiety is that your ideas, words, and resulting vision might not be any good to start with and wouldn't yield success even with a faithful follow-through.

Back in the early days of our browser projeci, Steve told us he wanted it to be fast. Don gave us his rule to realize this goal, never make the browser slower, as well as the Page Load Test, the means to accomplish it. Our browser team incorporated the PLT into our daily workflow, and we used the test results to measure and monitor our progress. Around a year later, when we were ready to release Safari, Steve could stand up on stage and, in a straightforward manner, tell the world what we had done. Our speedy browser lay at the end of a long chain linking inspiration to proposal to plan to process to product.

It may seem like a stretch to draw a comparison between winning football games in Green Bay and developing web browser software in Cupertino, but a significant part of attaining excellence in any field is closing the gap between the accidental and intentional, to achieve not just a *something* or even an *everything* but a *specific and well-chosen thing*, to take words and turn them into a vision, and then use the vision to spur the actions that create the results.

When I look back from our technology work to the coaching of Vince Lombardi, I see in his approach to football the same pursuit of clarity and perfection that we sought in our effort to make products at Apple. With his single-minded emphasis on the Power Sweep, and with the success the Packers enjoyed as a result, Vince Lombardi was the Steve Jobs of football coaches. Lombardi connected his words and his team's actions in football by focusing on one simple play, while at Apple, with our single-minded emphasis on never making the browser slower, we connected our words and actions in software by focusing on one simple rule.

5

The Hardest Problem

During my time at Apple, I worked on a certain class of hard problem, software challenges whose near-term solutions would have an immediate impact on our products. Soon after we shipped Safari, I found myself struggling with the hardest programming problem that I'd ever tackled. I also had a setback that nearly derailed my Apple career. By working through these difficulties, I learned an important lesson about collaboration, Apple style.

We initially released Safari as a beta, and within a day or two, we discovered a nasty bug that could delete data from people's computers. We rushed to publish a fix, but even with this glitch, the general view among Apple leadership was that our browser exceeded expectations. Scott Forstall was so pleased that he promoted Don to lead a new internet technologies group that included Safari, our email program, and iChat, our instant messaging software.

For me, the outcome was less spectacular. Don's promotion had left an opening for the Safari team manager. I put myself forward, but the job went to one of my teammates, Darin Adler. The decision-making process seemed too short and too secretive to me, given how hard I had worked on the browser and my founder's role on the team. Indeed, I had just one brief conversation with Don before the decision about his replacement came down.

I couldn't blame Darin for wanting the job, and he was certainly qualified, but I was upset nonetheless—so upset that I considered leaving Apple for Google. I sent an email to see if the web search company had any interest in hiring me, and they responded by inviting me in for two days of interviews. Unlike my brief conversation with Don, the interviewers at Google put me through my paces, sending me from engineer to engineer, with each asking me tough coding questions and watching me work out my answers on a whiteboard and on a laptop they provided for my use.

Apparently these interviews went well, because when the Google recruiter called to offer me a job a couple days later, she asked me my salary and stock expectations right over the phone, punctuating it with the phrase: "Think BIG!"

Unfortunately, at least from a financial perspective, I never got into naming numbers or thinking BIG!, because I told her that I had decided to remain at Apple.

By then Scott had heard that I was disappointed over the Safari management decision. He reached out to me. We met for a couple of hours, and he made it clear he didn't want me to go. He urged me to put the management change behind me, and, to help me do that, he said he wanted to know more about what made me tick. After we talked for a while, he concluded, correctly, that I liked projects much more than politics. Once he understood that, he said he might have an interesting project idea for me and that we would get together again in a few weeks to go over it.

That suited me. I really didn't want to leave Apple. I shared the company's focus on making great products, and I wanted to make more. Scott's overall vote of confidence in me meant more than any specific thing he said, and it made the difference in my choice to remain. I came away feeling that as long as I knew I'd be working with him and could reach out to him if I needed to, I'd be fine.

As promised, Scott called me in to his office a few weeks later. He began by describing how email was evolving—it was expanding beyond its origins as a text-only medium. Browser-based email services like Hotmail were fast becoming more popular, and Mac users were getting more and more email with web pages as the body of the message. We were still a decade away from ubiquitous social networks like Facebook, and back then, email was the best way to share digital content. Companies used email to send marketing brochures, spammers used email to directly target advertisements to the masses, and people used email to compile family vacation photo albums using apps like Apple iPhoto.

Scott said that more and more of these "rich" messages were coming through using web technology as the means to style the text and lay out the images. The trouble was, he told me, our Mac email program couldn't edit or reply to these web-based messages. Scott had a solution in mind. He suggested we could use WebKit, the core of our new browser code, to improve the email experience on the Mac. The technical challenge was that, as computer users, we *browse* the web. Other than filling out forms, as on ecommerce sites, we don't edit web pages while we read them. To make his plan work, he wanted me to enhance and adapt our browser code so people could treat the entirety of an emailed web page like it was a word processing document, editing the text and pictures in all the usual ways: typing new text, selecting passages with the mouse, deleting with the keyboard, cutting, copying, pasting, and so on. Scott explained that we were reaping the dividends of our investment in Safari and WebKit, since now we could decide for ourselves about the new web technology features we wanted in future Mac products. Web page editing for email was just such a technology. Scott asked me if I thought this sounded interesting.

I had never worked on a word processor but I didn't want to disappoint Scott, so I nodded and said, "Um . . . OK."

Scott treated this as an enthusiastic affirmation, and he pressed ahead to close the deal. He referred to Steve's fixation on email: Our CEO had continued sending email on a NeXT computer for several years after rejoining Apple because he thought the experience offered by his former company's software was superior.

I assured Scott that I knew about Steve's high standards—for email and for everything else. Scott went on to say that Steve wanted us to nail this web page editing feature, that The Man himself would be watching the progress on this email project, that if I did a great job, it would improve the email experience on our platform, and that I was the perfect person to do the work.

Invoking Steve was certainly part of Scott's sales pitch to get me to take on this web page editing work, but I had the sense that something else was going on, that Steve was breathing down Scott's neck. Scott not only wanted this work to get done—he *needed* it done.

This conversation illustrates an important aspect of how Apple software development worked: Leaders like Scott offered project opportunities to programmers like me. Scott was right when he suggested there weren't that many engineers who were in the position to make WebKit editing a reality. Steve and Scott wanted this new feature. If Apple was going to deliver it, someone had to "sign up" for the work and get it done.

I first encountered the term "signing up" in Tracy Kidder's *Soul of a New Machine,* a Pulitzer Prize–winning book on the quest to develop a new minicomputer at Data General Corporation in the late 1970s.[1] Kidder used the term to describe the moment one of the company's young and harried engineers took on the personal responsibility for delivering a project. At Apple, we didn't say "signing up" as formally or explicitly as Kidder tells us they did at Data General, but Kidder's stories had seeped into high tech over the years, and many Apple people had read his book (I sure did, more than once), so we were all aware of the signing up concept, and we lived it, even if we didn't say it.

The closest term we had in the Apple lexicon was more management speak: directly responsible individual (we pronounced it as D-R-I in conversation), the person who has to do whatever is necessary to develop a piece of hardware or software, some technology, some critically needed thing—the DRI was the person with their butt on the line.

When I was sitting there with Scott, I could have refused to sign up to become the DRI for his email editing idea, or asked for another project, or told Scott I was leaving for Google, but as long as I remained a software developer, a technologist, a maker of things, the project offers would change only in detail, not in kind, so I signed up.

"OK, Scott. I'll do the best I can."

He liked that answer.

That's how I became responsible for adding web page editing to WebKit, a technology I knew next to nothing about.

* * *

When I started this email editing work, hitting "reply" on an emailed web page caused the Mail program to try to stuff the web page into the simple email composer Apple Mail used in those days, a system that offered little more than basic text stylings (bold, italic, underline). Since this email composer wasn't a web browser, it couldn't interpret web pages properly. Replying to an emailed web page started you off with "On Jan 31 2003, so-and-so wrote:" but what followed all too often was scrambled and illegible web content.

My job was to prevent such garbled emails. To make that happen, I had to swap out the simple email composer from Apple Mail, install WebKit in its place, and make the change without anyone noticing. I had to make email composition work just as it had before for simple one-line messages and longer threaded conversations but ensure that Mail would no longer choke on web page email replies.

After a few days of thinking, I figured out where I should begin programming for my new project. I decided to add an *insertion point,* also called a *caret* or *cursor,* the blinking line that follows you around as you edit text. I had rudimentary insertion point demos working within a month, but it took me almost a year to get WebKit editing working well enough that I could begin to edit the web pages I typically received in my email inbox. This was longer than I had expected, but for once in my Apple career, the schedule minders weren't breathing down my neck (for reasons I didn't know, and I wasn't eager to find out).

There were a host of editing features to add, including typing and deleting text, support for undoing these operations, and testing that none of my editing additions slowed down web page load performance. Even though I had made good progress after those many months of concentrated effort, I was still tripping over bad bugs with the first feature I added: the placement, movement, and behavior of the blinking insertion point.

Before starting on this project, I had never thought much about the insertion point as I sent texts, composed emails, posted to internet message boards, and wrote longer reports and presentations in programs like Keynote, Word, and PowerPoint. I was finding out that this familiar feature belied the underlying complexity of word processors and the subtle behaviors they exhibit.

To illustrate the nature of my difficulties, consider these two behavioral rules for the insertion point, one simple and one complicated:

Simple Rule: The insertion point stops blinking while you type and resumes blinking a fraction of a second after you cease tapping keys.

Complicated Rule: In a normal block of text, the end of a line can hold an infinite number of spaces. This might seem absurd, but this is the rule that makes left-aligned text possible. Without it, blocks of text with multiple spaces on the end of the line might become "ragged" on the left margin. To see this rule work, position the insertion point after the last character on a line in the middle of a paragraph of text that is broken into several lines. Start typing spaces. Once the insertion point reaches the end of the line where text breaks into the next line, adding yet more spaces moves neither the text nor the insertion point. Additional spaces are collapsed into nothing. To see all your spaces, resize the window or cause the text to reflow in some other way by adding or deleting characters.

A "COMPLICATED" INSERTION POINT RULE

Four score and seven years ago our fathers brought forth, upon this continent, a new nation, conceived in Liberty, and dedicated to the proposition|
that all men are created equal.

[space] [space] [space] [space] [space]

Position the insertion point after "proposition". Type several spaces.

Four score and seven years ago our fathers brought forth, upon this continent, a new nation, conceived in Liberty, and dedicated to the proposition|
that all men are created equal.

The newly-added spaces are not visible. An infinite number can fit on the end of the line.

Four score and seven years ago our fathers brought forth, upon this continent, a new nation, conceived in Liberty, and dedicated to the proposition |that all men are created equal.

The spaces added at the end of the line after "proposition" only become visible after resizing the window, or if the text reflows due to edits elsewhere.

Before I started on this WebKit editing project, I had an internalized sense that these rules were making my word processing experience work as I expected, and I'm sure I would have noticed right away if either of these rules suddenly disappeared—for example, why is my left-aligned text now ragged on the left margin? Yet I didn't understand these rules intellectually. Now that it was my job to make WebKit function as a full-featured word processor, I no longer had the luxury of getting by on my built-up intuitive feel for typing and editing in email. I had to become an expert in all the nuances of word processors. There's no programmer's handbook on this topic, so I had to run experiments to discover the rules on my own. I needed to come to grips with the letter and spirit of all these rules, both simple and complicated. In my studies, I spent many hours poking and prodding different word processors, Microsoft Word, the Apple Mail composer, and BBEdit, the editor I used to write my programs—testing, tapping, typing, clicking. Little by little, I learned about more rules and how to write code to implement them. As I did so, I became stuck.

I couldn't get the insertion point to behave correctly in all cases. Most times it worked as expected, but then it would suddenly misbehave. Sometimes the blinking line would pin itself to one spot and cease to move. Sometimes it would disappear altogether after I clicked with the mouse. Sometimes it would skip characters, or lines, or jump around seemingly at random as I typed. Sometimes tapping a key would make it reappear, and sometimes not. My insertion point woes were the worst kind of bugs a coder can have, since the bad behavior didn't always recur if I backed up and took the same steps again.

Programmers have a name for such defects. We evoke the uncertainty principle from quantum mechanics and the man, Werner Heisenberg, who developed it. My insertion point glitches were "heisenbugs." And fixing insertion point heisenbugs was the hardest programming problem I ever tried to solve.

To give a complete technical explanation of the problems I was wrestling with to make my insertion code produce the correct visual outcome, I would need to describe the format used to define web pages, HTML (Hypertext Markup Language), plus more esoteric-sounding things such as DOM node structures, tree traversal algorithms, and more. Instead, I'll offer an analogy. Consider the following:

A customer walks up to a counter in a bakery to place an order for a customized cake. The customer says, "I would like a cake that says 'Happy Birthday' and, below that, 'Tom.'"

How do these two people confirm to each other that they've gotten everything right? It becomes even more difficult if I strip away some of the helpful punctuation and capitalization to more closely mimic the experience of two people speaking to each other:

"I would like a cake that says happy birthday and below that tom."

We shouldn't be too surprised that, at least some of the time, there's miscommunication about how this cake should look. Maybe the customer didn't speak clearly. Maybe the baker suffers from a chronic deficit of common sense or has simply had a long day. Whenever any such breakdowns happen, the result can be a jocular jumble.

In my sample order, only three of the words of the customer request—"Happy," "Birthday," and "Tom"—are supposed to be written on the cake, but there also was a positioning directive in there, and all this knowledge is encoded implicitly in the original spoken request. Most times people can figure it out from context, but sometimes they get it wrong, as is shown by a Google image search for "birthday cake fails."

Word processors are like birthday cake orders. When you type in a word processor, then select a word and make it bold, then click someplace else and type some more, you create a stream of data that directly indicates how the text should look. The word processor must keep track of your actions, like a conscientious and efficient bakery counter clerk, to make sure your document always looks like you expect.

In my effort to make the insertion point move correctly, my problem was with HTML, the web page data format. The word "markup" in Hypertext Markup Language refers to the way data

is interleaved with *metadata,* information about the data. Here's a simple example of some HTML and its rendered result:

Some <b>bold text, some <i>bold italic</i></b>, and some plain.

Some **bold text, some *bold italic*, and some plain.**

As you can see, as in the birthday cake order the customer spoke to the clerk, the text and the styling cues run together. In HTML, it's not always easy to tell the markup from the content. Data and metadata are mixed. Here is a more complicated and realistic example I cribbed from the Wikipedia page for the white-naped xenopsaris,[2] a small South American bird, with the HTML source followed by its rendering:

```
<p>The <b>white-naped xenopsaris</b> (<i>Xenopsaris albinucha</i>),
also known as the <b>reed becard</b> and <b>white-naped becard</b>,
is a <a href="/wiki/Species" title="Species">species</a> of
<a href="/wiki/Tyranni" title="Tyranni">suboscine</a> bird in the
<a href="/wiki/Family_(biology)" title="Family (biology)">family</a>
<a href="/wiki/Tityridae" title="Tityridae">Tityridae</a>, the only
member of the <a href="/wiki/Genus" title="Genus">genus</a> <i>
<b>Xenopsaris</b></i>.
```

The **white-naped xenoparis** (*Xenopsaris albinucha*), also known as the **reed becard** and **white-naped becard**, is a <u>species</u> of <u>suboscine</u> bird in the <u>family Tityridae</u>, the only member of the <u>genus</u> *Xenoparis*.

Which parts of the stream of HTML text above are visualized in the rendering of the text below it and which parts are just styling cues, links, or other not-to-be rendered data? Where does the markup begin and where does it end? It begins with understanding angle bracket characters (< and >), but it's more complicated than that. Indeed, my primary challenge on my WebKit editing project was dealing with HTML, a mixed-together format that I had trouble turning into a general-purpose data representation for word processing. I couldn't figure out an efficient way to move back and forth between this data and its correct visualization, and if I couldn't do that, I couldn't make the insertion point blink in the right place.

I spent months trying to develop a way to disentangle content from markup, and as time passed, I became increasingly frustrated that I couldn't solve the problem. I added more cases to handle specific sequences of HTML. I did detailed analyses of my bugs in an attempt to discern patterns in the defects. I spent weeks concentrating on the problem in my office at Apple, and when that didn't yield sufficient progress, I started coding at home during evenings and weekends. None of it worked.

I was stuck.

Eventually I went to Don. I'd felt lingering disappointment that he hadn't chosen me to succeed him as the leader of the Safari team, but despite that, our longer-term friendship had held, and even though he was no longer my direct manager, I continued to consult him when I was in tough spots. I sure needed his help with my insertion point problem. I confessed to him that I had been puzzling over my bugs by myself for a while, and it was time for me to get some advice. While I had been making progress on the other editing features I needed to deliver, I was starting to worry that my WebKit editing effort might fail altogether because of my inability to write rock-solid insertion point code.

Don suggested I meet with two colleagues on our web browser team, Darin Adler, now my manager, and Trey Matteson, a temporary contractor helping us improve our code. Both were excellent programmers with far more than my eight years of professional coding experience. Darin's work on Safari actually was his second stint at Apple. His first was back in the 1980s, when he led a software architecture team for System 7, a note-worthy operating system release in the history of the Mac. Trey was an early developer on AppKit at NeXT, code that was now part of the software backbone of app development at Apple. Don thought these two fellows had the know-how to help me with my hard technical problem.

In my office with Darin and Trey a day or two later, I stood up at my whiteboard. Both my colleagues were focused and in-tent on listening. Darin showed it by fidgeting, rocking back and forth on the hind legs of the IKEA chair I kept for guests, while Trey sat still and upright on a spare office chair I had wheeled in from the hallway. The scene must have looked something like a three-man version of the chalkboard sessions Vince Lombardi ran for his football players, except that the famous coach's confi-dence was replaced by my confusion. I proceeded to describe my insertion point problem as best I could, filling the whiteboard with diagrams. I covered what I knew about how to position and move an insertion point in web content. I went over the details of trying to use HTML as a word processing data format. I listed all the cases I couldn't handle and the inconsistent comings and goings of my heisenbugs. I laid out everything, and throughout, I made it abundantly clear I was stuck and didn't know what to do next.

Darin and Trey asked questions, and after about a half hour, they had located the root of my insertion point problem: I was spending too much time thinking about data and not enough thinking about the visuals. I had gotten so wrapped around the axle trying to decipher HTML that I had neglected to write code that guaranteed the results I was trying to produce.

When I described my attempts to move the insertion point in a specific case—responding to a tap on the right arrow key— Darin and Trey noted that I didn't have a single piece of code responsible for making this entire operation work correctly from the user's point of view. Sure, I had code to detect key taps, and code to track the current insertion point position, and code to yield information about the HTML structure around the insertion point, and code to navigate around angle brackets. I also had a loosely coordinated method of using these code components to yield insertion point movement. They told me this wasn't good enough. They said I needed an authoritative piece of software that said "Move the insertion point one position to the right starting from where it is now," one that handled both the complications of HTML data and the end result the user would see.

Lacking that, Darin and Trey told me, I was like a discombobulated bakery store worker using a pad of sticky notes to scribble down birthday orders on a succession of little yellow slips, hoping I could later consult these scraps and produce perfect cakes. They said my stack of coding sticky notes was too unstructured and too disordered to make sure my insertion point visuals would always come out right.

They suggested that I create the software equivalent of a birthday cake ordering form, one thoughtfully and carefully designed, with a specific space for every piece of information I needed to produce the proper insertion point behavior. They zeroed in on defects in my code, such as when the insertion point sometimes disappeared. They said that should never happen, just like a bakery should never have a finished cake ready for pickup but no knowledge of who ordered it. My code needed explicit steps that ensured the insertion point always stayed visible—regardless of the complexity of the HTML—just like a bakery clerk needs to take down contact information accurately when a customer orders a cake.

When it came time to discuss a solution, they told me that I should clean up my code. Over months, as I struggled, I had scattered special-case insertion point functions throughout my project. They told me that was a mistake, but their specific software prescription—to gather the code back together into a single C++ class, which they proposed we call VisiblePosition—was about more than tidiness. It represented an important technical insight: When software behavior is mysterious, get more organized. My insertion point code needed to be as businesslike as a baker looking at a properly filled out order form to determine the correct words to write on a cake.

After our meeting, I did exactly as they'd advised. I gathered my code together and added a more explicit focus on the visual outcome of the HTML machinations I already had in abundance. Although my insertion point woes didn't disappear right away, I started making progress eliminating my heisenbugs.

Why were Darin and Trey able to see this way ahead when I couldn't? After all, I made C++ classes all the time. It's a common programming task. That said, at the time I was juggling other technical problems in other parts of the project that I skipped over in this account for the sake of brevity. Yet, when I did finally ask Darin and Trey for help, I was able to explain all the issues clearly. Darin and Trey combined my explanations with their fresh perspective, and, with their surpassing skill as software architects, they quickly saw a solution that had eluded me and were able to back it up with a general principle that justified why they were making their suggestion.

Although I was stuck and they were skillful, my state of mind was also important in how our meeting played out. If I had reached out for help earlier, I might have felt more defensive in such a technical review with my colleagues. I have pride in my craft and in my ability to solve hard problems, and although I always think of myself as being willing to collaborate, that doesn't always come across as clearly as it might. If I hadn't been so desperately stuck, I might not have been as open to the advice Darin and Trey offered, and I might have signaled this in subtle ways.

Indeed, what if I had been in a different state of mind? What if I had drawn fewer diagrams and droned on in a monotone, and the attention of my colleagues had started to drift? What if I had demonstrated any kind of reluctance to listen to their feedback—perhaps by standing cross-armed when I wasn't busy sketching? What if Darin or Trey were sitting with me only because the idea had been suggested by Don, who served as a manager over all of us? What if I had harbored a long-term grudge against Darin for beating me out of the Safari manager position, and he sensed that I did? If any of these social obstructions had gotten in the way, this technical meeting might not have turned out so well, and I might have remained stuck.

I didn't. After our meeting finished up, I began to act directly and unequivocally on the advice Darin and Trey had given me. I followed the software prescription just as they had suggested. Then, in follow-up code change reviews with them, I made demos that showed how their advice was leading to specific bug fixes—making the insertion point move stepwise where it used to skip and keeping it visible where it used to vanish.

These subsequent interactions had an effect I didn't expect. Once it was clear to Darin and Trey that their advice was leading to obvious improvements in my code, they appeared to like it. Even though the technical work to make the insertion point behave better was still my responsibility, they could share in the turnaround they helped bring about. My bug fixes were now something we could talk about in detail in hallway conversations and over lunch, and our collaboration gave them the technical grounding they needed to have opinions and make further suggestions.

I had succeeded in getting my colleagues invested in my insertion point behavior work, not just by asking for their help in a single meeting and saying thanks when it was finished but by demonstrating through my ongoing actions in code changes, demo reviews, and lunchtime chats that their advice had mattered to me. Getting the insertion point to behave correctly wasn't just my project anymore. It was now *our* project.

This points to the more general lesson I took from my WebKit editing work: People matter more than programming. This may sound trite, but many coders find it easier to get along with computers than colleagues, and there's a tendency in Silicon Valley to view every question as having a technological answer. Yet, if Scott hadn't found the right words to say to me in the wake of the Safari management change, I might have gone off to Google, and I might have never signed up for the WebKit editing project at all. If Don, Darin, and I had been unable to continue working together because of my feelings over that same management change, or if I had been too prideful to make productive use of the advice I got from Darin and Trey, I might have remained stuck with a flaky insertion point, and my WebKit word processing project might have failed. The project didn't fail, and even though I designed all the concepts for HTML editing, and I wrote virtually every line of code we shipped to customers to bring them web-enabled email composition, I can't claim to have done the project by myself.

As a programmer and self-professed geek, possessed of a typical geek programmer's communication skills, it was a revelation to me that both the setting and the solution to my hardest technical problem turned as much on the social side of my job as it did on the software side.

6

The Keyboard Derby

At Apple, there was never much time to savor success. Steve Jobs explained this aspect of the company ethos in an interview with NBC *Nightly News* anchor Brian Williams, on the occasion of the opening of the Apple Store on Fifth Avenue in Manhattan in 2006. Williams asked Steve where he "fit in the American family of thinkers and inventors." At first, Steve attempted to brush off the question, but when Williams pressed him, Steve said: "I think if you do something and it turns out pretty good, then you should go do something else wonderful, not dwell on it for too long. Just figure out what's next."[1]

That's what I did as my WebKit word processing project started winding down. I started to figure out what was next. I didn't do very well, but I found Steve's approach could work as well after a failure as he said it could after a success.

After I finished up HTML editing, I went back to meet with Scott Forstall to talk with him about my next assignment. I told him it still bothered me that I hadn't gotten the Safari manager position two years earlier, and I asked for the chance to manage one of the other programming teams in his department.

At the time, there was an opening for manager of Sync Services, the team responsible for data synchronization between Macs and Apple's cloud services, which were then called .Mac.* I asked for the job. Scott agreed. So did Henri Lamiraux, who was, at this time, reporting to Scott and leading the group of teams that included sync.

I liked the people on my new team, and sync was technically challenging, but very soon, I was miserable in my new job. Why? Mostly because I was unprepared for the change in my daily routine. I went from writing software every day to worrying about my team. My schedule was always full of meetings. I had to navigate cross-functional relationships with other teams related to sync, and that involved much more politicking than I was expecting or was used to. I hadn't realized how much I relied on writing code to feel productive and happy. My programming skill suddenly didn't matter, and I didn't have an intuitive sense for what I needed to do to be successful as a manager. I had taken the job for the wrong reason. It was my poorly judged attempt to make up for the missed management opportunity on Safari.

I also began to see that not all Apple projects were created equal. One day I ran into the fellow who handled the marketing for some of the products in Scott's organization, including Safari. He had always worked directly with Don on the messaging

---

* Back before there were iPhones and iPads, sync was mostly a technology for people who habitually used multiple Macs, perhaps a desktop at home and a laptop for working on the go. Also note that Sync Services updated data only between Macs. It never handled syncing music between your Mac and your iPod. That was a different technology developed by the iPod and iTunes teams.

for the web browser, but I saw him in the Safari hallway often, so we stopped to chat.

"Hey, Ken. How do you like your new management job?"

"Hi, Kurt. It's good," I lied. Yet I thought this brief chat might have a silver lining. I made my pitch. "So, now that I'm managing Sync Services, maybe you and I can collaborate on the marketing for it."

When Kurt heard my suggestion, his expression changed. He gave a nervous laugh and then he broke the bad news, letting me in on a fact that was obvious to him but about which I was oblivious.

"Ken, we don't market sync. We don't really consider it a . . . well . . . a customer-facing technology."

Kurt seemed half embarrassed for himself and half for me. I knew immediately that "customer-facing" was Kurt's euphemism for "important," at least from his perspective in the marketing department.

This viewpoint counts for more than you might think. Apple is customer-focused. The company always sought to give people convincing reasons to buy its products. If the marketing department wasn't interested in telling people about sync, then the feature was something Apple felt it needed to do, not necessarily something that it wanted to do or was excited about doing.

I didn't know how to respond to Kurt, and I let our conversation trail off. I walked on, picked up my lunch, returned to my office, and closed the door. I stared at my schedule in the calendar program on my Mac, wondering whether I could be happy in the long term working on behind-the-scenes technology that wouldn't be the reason why customers bought Apple products.

Around this time, I started to hear mumblings about a new super-secret project that was just getting under way somewhere in Scott's department. I couldn't find out for sure what it was, and the information on the grapevine was sparse, which meant it might be something big. Was it a new product? A new piece of hardware that might need some software? I didn't know, but I was positive about one thing: I felt lost in my new job as the sync manager.

Few people suspected how unhappy I was, but my wife knew. She always encouraged me to keep an open mind about where I could work, that I was married to her, not to Apple. She suggested I might contact Google again. Over the July 4 weekend, only three months after accepting my role on sync, we decided. I would go tell Henri that I was done being a manager. I would tell him that I had made a mistake and that it would be better for everyone if I just admitted it and moved on.

When Henri and I met, I told him that I wanted out of the sync job right away. I was adamant. Looking back now, that wasn't fair. I should have given him some sort of timeline, some period of transition, but I didn't. Despite that, Henri remained calm. He said he was completely surprised and that he needed more information to take to Scott so they could decide what to do. It was then that I mentioned the rumor of the new super-secret project, and I suggested that if I could transfer to that, I might not quit Apple for Google.

When I said that, Henri lurched his head backward—the kind of snap response people make when they hear something they can't quite believe. By floating this transfer idea and threatening to quit, it must have sounded to Henri like I was playing a hard angle, but I honestly wasn't. I looked at this question like a programmer would, as a binary issue. Either I wanted to do the sync manager job wholeheartedly, or I didn't want to do it at all.

Obviously, inevitably, I wound up in a meeting with Scott. I told him I wanted out of the sync job with the same resolve I had used with Henri, even though it was becoming increasingly clear that my approach wasn't going over well. I said that managing the sync team wasn't for me, and if I was going to stay at Apple, I needed to work on something else. I apologized. I offered to resign. Scott told me to slow down. From his perspective, I had gotten the management opportunity I said I wanted, and now I was asking for something else just a few months later. I had signed up for sync. "Unsigning up" just wasn't done. Scott wanted to understand and help me, but he wasn't convinced I knew what I wanted, and as I think back, he was right to have his doubts. He asked me to wait before I made any decisions, and with that, our meeting was over.

A couple days after that, Henri called me into his office. He closed the door. We sat down. He asked me to sign a piece of paper. It was a nondisclosure agreement, an NDA, a legal agreement that, in the typical Apple formulation, forbade me to talk about the secrets named in the document to anyone who I wasn't sure had also signed the same NDA. I was already under a blanket NDA from the day I started at Apple, but I guessed what might happen if I signed the new one in front of me.

I didn't hesitate.

Then Henri told me. "Yeah, we're making a cell phone. Its code name is Purple."

Just like that, I had joined the biggest super-secret project at the company, perhaps in Apple's whole history. I felt a mixture of guilt and euphoria. If I'd banked points with my work on Safari and WebKit, my account was now back to zero. While my relations with Scott seemed at level almost immediately, Henri remained more skeptical, certainly at first, and the sideways glances he shot my way over the next few weeks told me that my balance with him had dipped into the red.

About two weeks after I signed the NDA, I moved onto a hallway with the rest of the new Purple software engineering team, about six or eight of us. The choice of hallway wasn't a coincidence. We were close to Scott, and he would be the executive in charge of our smartphone development group.

We were also just one badge-access door away from the Human Interface (HI) team. They were the designers who would imbue Purple software with a spirit, from concepts and principles to animations and icons. Those of us on the programming team were responsible for supplying the sinew, by adding on the code, algorithms, and apps. Together, we had to bring our touchscreen operating system to life and give our phone a software personality.

A new door and badge reader was soon fitted to the entrance of our programming hallway too, which meant that Apple employees who weren't disclosed on the smartphone initiative could no longer wander over to our offices on a whim, poke their heads in, and see what was happening as we got started on Purple. We now inhabited our own hallway of secrets.

I was reunited with a couple of my colleagues from the Safari project, including Richard Williamson, who became my manager. Richard reported to Henri, who also left the sync project, albeit in a less dramatic way than I did. As the Purple project got started, Scott and Henri starting plucking programmers from across the Apple software organization. All of us, including Henri and the HI team led by Greg Christie, reported to Scott, who, as always, had an inside line to Steve Jobs.

We planned to build our phone software around a technology we called *multitouch*, a hardware and software system that could sense and respond to taps and slides on a transparent touchscreen that could also display colorful content underneath your fingers. Experiments with multitouch had been going on inside Apple for some time, but until I joined the team it was a black project completely hidden from my view.

Now I needed to know.

During my visit to the HI studio to get my first look at multi-touch, Bas Ording took me through an interactive demo he had made, as always, in Adobe Director. On his desk, he had a device we called a Wallaby, and this phone-sized experimental device was how Bas developed and tested his touchscreen demo. Prototype hardware met prototype software on the Wallaby, a multitouch display designed to give an approximation of the correct form factor of our smartphone and provide the right feel in your grip as you touched the screen. The Wallaby was tethered to a Mac through a supplementary hardware board and an umbilical cable about a quarter-inch thick. The Wallaby was only a screen. The Mac supplied the computing power, and various other connectors ran here and there. All this gear provided the hardware support to make the prototype software come alive. Bas picked up the Wallaby display, and as he tapped and swiped, he showed me the rudiments of an Apple-style touchscreen user interface system, including an intuitive, row-and-column home screen icon launcher program called SpringBoard and a fluid inertial scrolling scheme that bounced playfully when he reached the end of a list.[2] Today we're all familiar with how these things work, but on that day, I got my first look at the future of personal technology.

Impressive as it was, the software Bas showed me wasn't a firm base for long-term development, since there was no direct engineering path from a Director demo to a shippable product. We would need a software infrastructure built on a hardcore programming language like C++ or Objective-C, and my arrival on the Purple team had come on the heels of Steve's decision about what that foundation would be.

Richard, who had been working on Purple for a couple months longer than I, filled me in on the details. He told me that they'd considered the iPod software platform, since it already ran on handheld devices, but they questioned whether it could be expanded into a sophisticated system that could run multiple apps at once. They'd also thought about using the full-featured AppKit framework we used to develop programs for the Mac, since it provided menus, windows, and a collection of other user interface necessities, but they wondered if they could shrink it to run on the more constrained hardware platform of a smartphone. They'd thought of using WebKit, which would have meant constructing the user interface system from a set of elaborate web pages, but they were worried about ease of programmability. They'd also considered developing a brand-new touch-centric user interface system from scratch.

All these efforts had been going on in parallel, but after a couple weeks of investigation, the AppKit and WebKit options were deemed impractical and fell by the wayside.

This period had been reminiscent of the early days of the web browser project, when we had to choose a technology direction from an array of options. But Purple was different. The stakes were higher—Steve Jobs was watching obsessively. As a new hardware product with the potential to rival and cannibalize the sales of the hottest Apple product of the day, the iPod, there had been an intense competition to be at the center of what might be the next big thing. Tony Fadell, the senior vice president of iPod development, had wanted the phone software to be in his domain. Scott Forstall thought he could do better, and these two had engaged in an executive-level contest to own the future of Purple software development.

Scott won the tussle by assigning Henri and a couple of software engineers to develop a platform that borrowed as much from the Mac as possible but replaced AppKit with a brand-new multitouch-aware user interface system called UIKit. Henri's skunk works engineering team created demos for inertial scrolling and SpringBoard—the key user interface innovations Bas had shown me on the Wallaby—as well as an early demo of Safari, all running on a product you could carry in your pocket. With these demos, Scott made a compelling case that his software team could squeeze the software essentials of the Mac onto a smartphone. Steve agreed.

Other decisions followed on from that. More programmers were brought onto the Purple project, like me. Scott soon chose my WebKit code for all editable text on our smartphone, in programs like Notes, and in Contacts, Calendar, and Mail—everywhere there was a blinking insertion point—so I got started developing touchscreen text editing. For Purple, I had to adapt my editing code to a hardware platform that didn't have a mouse and a physical keyboard, but experimenting with touchscreen text editing felt like blazing new trails, and I was happy to do it. My first actual progress was a demo to edit the web address in the location bar in our smartphone version of Safari, and I didn't need to wait long to show it off.

Once or twice every week, Scott led a tour of the software hallway to see the latest Purple demos. A dozen programmers, designers, and managers crammed into our one-person offices. We huddled around Scott, who held the latest Wallaby prototype hardware in front of him in the now-familiar two-hands, thumbs-free grip. He sat at the center of the presentation and acted as chief reviewer and decider. We all craned our necks to see what he was looking at, as he went through updates on apps, designs, and thoughts for making a computing system built around touch.

Even when demos went well, there was always a steady flow of feedback, suggestions for changes, impressions on how the software might behave differently. Everyone spoke up. Demos were an open forum for exchanging ideas about how an interaction might look or function better. When demos went poorly, as sometimes happened, there was the same stream of comments and constructive criticism. There was never any finger-pointing; however, there was an expectation that new demos would include a response to the feedback from previous demos. This was the one essential demo expectation: progress.

Our software leaders—Scott, Henri, Greg, and Kim Vorrath, the program manager for Purple who had primary responsibility for monitoring the development schedule—were always gauging headway. They repeatedly asked themselves the same basic questions during these periodic reviews: Does this demo close the prototype-to-product gap, even a little? Are we seeing enough positive change over last time? Is this technology or app on track?

The demos rolled on, with early versions of our app-launching animations followed by font size tests that gauged how much text we might fit on the screen while still remaining legible, followed by prototypes for apps like Contacts and Calendar. Good sessions mixed in with the not-as-good ones.

Around September 2005, there was an especially difficult demo for the onscreen software keyboard. Although the engineers who made this demo, Scott Herz and Wayne Westerman, were responsible for so much that was good in the shipping smartphone—Scott created SpringBoard from scratch and Wayne was one of the key inventors of multitouch—this latest keyboard demo wasn't going well. I remember Scott Forstall sitting in an office chair, leaning forward, cupping the Wallaby screen in his hands as he attempted to use the keyboard demo on offer.

Try as he might, Scott repeatedly failed to thumb-type anything intelligible. The onscreen keyboard produced not just wrong words but babble. Scott kept trying, deleting backward and then typing again. Every effort ended in gobbledygook. Eventually, Scott shifted the Wallaby to his left hand and tilted it to a near forty-five-degree angle to his face. Holding it closer, he focused intently on the screen and slowly moved his right index finger toward the **S** key, intending to type the first letter of his name. He couldn't. The keys were too small, and the software was hopelessly confused. No matter what he tried, Scott couldn't type "Scott." He called an end to the demo, put down the Wallaby, and the demo group moved on.

A day or two later, we were in for a surprise. Henri called all the Purple programmers out of our offices. By this time, there were about fifteen of us, and when we all were gathered in the hallway, Henri made an announcement. He told us to stop what we were doing, to set our current projects aside, to temporarily halt all work on Safari, Mail, SpringBoard, Notes—everything. Henri told us that Scott was pushing a big Purple pause button. He wanted everyone to start making keyboards right away. The recent "difficult" keyboard demo had raised concerns up and down the management chain. It was critical for us to have a software keyboard for our touchscreen smartphone, and the official word had now come down: Progress was too slow.

Remember back to this time. In the fall of 2005, as we were busy on Purple in complete secrecy, the BlackBerry was enjoying great success in the market. Its "CrackBerry" nickname was a nod to the addictive way people kept up on their email and messages by typing on its well-designed hardware keyboard with its little chiclet keys.[3]

Our Purple phone wouldn't have a hardware keyboard. There were no prototypes in the Industrial Design studio that included anything like a BlackBerry-style keyboard. The Purple concept was built around a large touchscreen and a minimum number of fixed buttons. Apple had bet everything on a software keyboard. When it came to typing, plastic keys would give way to pixels. As a software team and as a company, we were all in. However, when it came to figuring out how to type on a flat display without tactile keys, we weren't figuring it out fast enough.

Henri looked at his software team assembled in the hallway and said, "Starting from now, you're all keyboard engineers." He concluded by saying we would get together for a demo derby once we had a collection of new software prototypes to show.

As I listened to Henri, I wondered whether this was a last-ditch effort to get keyboard development back on track. What if we couldn't? Would Purple be canceled? Henri didn't come out and say it that way, but he didn't have to. In all my years at Apple, we'd never before halted a fifteen-person project to focus everyone on a single problem.

While we were still standing in the hallway, I saw an image in my mind, the dashboard of a car, and this all-hands meeting caused one of the yellow warning lights to pop on. Underneath the now-lit indicator bulb, it said: *Important.* After the meeting broke up, I went right back to my office and, for the first time, I started thinking seriously about typing on touchscreens.

I don't know what my Purple teammates thought or pictured in their minds, but their response was immediate as well. Our hallway started buzzing, first with ideas, then, within days, our first keyboard prototypes. Most of these early efforts were practical and were modeled on shrunk-down laptop keyboards, with many variations that moved keys to new locations to aid in usability. Some of the ideas were fanciful, like a Morse code–inspired keyboard that entered letters by combining taps and slides to mimic dots and dashes. One prototype looked like a piano—a marvelous play on the word "keyboard"—where you pressed multiple keys at once to type out words as if you were playing chords in a tune.

I made my own keyboards too, and like my colleagues, my initial tries were quick software sketches. There was none of the spell checking, word prediction, or keyboard software assistance that has become familiar. Back then, those features would have seemed like moon rockets when we were still trying to make a slingshot. Instead of even attempting any advanced concepts, I tested whether it might be easier to target individual letter keys if they were shaped like interlocking puzzle pieces. When I showed my prototypes to Richard Williamson, he wasn't impressed.

"Your keyboards are like everybody else's, and they don't work. Everyone is making their keys too small, and they're too hard to tap," he told me. "*The keys need to be bigger.*"

My own fat thumbs quickly confirmed what Richard was saying. Back before touchscreen smartphones became ubiquitous, a new kind of user interaction was involved in picking up a handheld device and aiming at an array of software buttons, all closely packed together, each one smaller than a fingertip, and with nothing tactile to tell you whether you'd hit or missed your target. Now we're accustomed to tapping away on touchscreens, but in these early prototyping days, all of us on the Purple hallway felt a twinge of apprehension when it came to tapping tiny targets on a Wallaby, because at the crucial moment, your finger covered up the thing you were trying to tap, and you couldn't see what you were doing.

This was the problem Richard wanted us to solve. He proposed using keys much bigger than your fingertip, with three or four large keys per row rather than the dozen or more found on a shrunk-down standard computer keyboard. This was easy enough to do, but obviously, such a keyboard couldn't include enough keys for every letter to have its own. So we started ganging up multiple letters on each key as they did on flip phone keypads and developing various means to choose the correct letter: sliding, double taps, long presses, and others.

Richard made prototypes to explore this idea. I responded with my own, which I called the Blob keyboard.[4]

It was easier to target keys on these big-key keyboards, but taking more screen space for the keyboard left much less room above for user content than we had been planning for in the earliest prototypes.

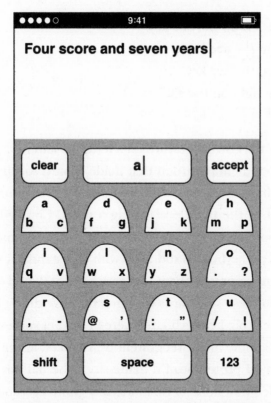

My "Blob" keyboard prototype. Tapping a key entered
the letter at the top. Entering the letters on the bottom
sides of the key required a slide to that side.

Even more important from a user interaction standpoint, everyone had trouble with the quick letter-by-letter decision to tap or swipe. Think about it: To type on a keyboard, whether an old-style manual model, or an IBM Selectric, or the keyboard on your laptop, every press on a character key enters that character. Press, press, press. In contrast, Richard-style Purple prototype keyboards with multiple letters on each key required everyone to think about every letter. With my Blob keyboard, typing a common word like "bank" required a sequence of different gestures:

- Swipe left on the **abc** key.
- Tap on the **abc** key.
- Tap on the **nyz** key.
- Swipe right on the **ejk** key.

Picking the correct gesture on a letter-by-letter basis created an additional mental burden that made it hard to think. When I tried Richard's big-key keyboards and he tried mine, we often got lost in the middle of typing a word. Coupled with the redistribution of letters into unfamiliar layouts—almost all of our prototype keyboards did away with the standard QWERTY arrangement—none of them was easy to use. Would we get accustomed to these keyboards with practice? We didn't know, but for sure, these big-key keyboards weren't instant successes.

After a couple more weeks went by, I looked at the five complete keyboard prototypes I'd made since the hallway meeting, and I decided that none of them was any good. I scrapped them, but I wasn't starting over from square one. I'd taken away a few lessons:

1. Big keys were easier to tap. Richard was right.
2. Rearranging the letters on the keyboard was a bad idea. Sticking with the common QWERTY arrangement made it easier for people to find the right letters without having to hunt around.
3. Keys should be tap only. Having to choose different finger gestures on a key-by-key basis was too hard.

I decided to make a new keyboard based on these principles, and I thought there was still more unrealized potential to reduce the mental burden. I wanted to make a keyboard that demanded

My big-key, tap-only, dictionary-assisted keyboard prototype.

less attention from people as they tapped, a keyboard that allowed people to think more about their typing and less about futzing with the touchscreen and the user interface.

Here was my concept: a big-key QWERTY keyboard that displayed multiple letters per key but that offloaded the decision of picking the letters to the computer. No more swipes or slides. Typing a three-letter word would always take three taps, a five-letter word would always take five taps, and so on.

To type the word "light," you would tap the keys that displayed those letters:

Then the keyboard would figure out you meant "light," since that was the most sensible word with that combination of keys and letters. To make this work, I needed a word list, a dictionary. I also needed some software to access this lexicon to make a "most sensible word" determination.

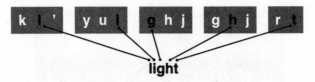

The most sensible word for this succession of keys is "light."

The only problem was that I had no idea how to make a dictionary. At times like that, it was great to be an Apple employee. The company had an immense back catalog of projects, research, and resources. I poked around. I spelunked through dark corners of long-disused directories of software stored in

Apple archives. I gathered information from various sources, and I assembled a rudimentary list of English words.

Over the next week or two, I wrote some code to take keyboard taps, perform a dictionary lookup, and update the display with suggested words. I struggled with the dictionary code, and even though Richard helped me improve the speed of my dictionary lookups with a couple clever programming ideas, I was barely ready when I got a calendar invitation. This was the call to bring our prototype keyboards to a group meeting where Scott would try them all out. If he liked one, he would declare a winner.

Our program manager, Kim Vorrath, organized this important meeting, and she circulated a plan for a demo that called for all the keyboard derby participants to build their prototypes into a common program, one that would make it easier for Scott to jump from one software prototype to the next without a custom procedure to cue up each entrant. This was a fine idea, but I had too much trouble compiling my dictionary to adapt my code to fit into Kim's demo switcher. I decided to have a nonconforming demo that functioned properly, rather than the opposite, and when derby day came around, I was the only one who had failed to alter my demo. I would need to run my code separately from everyone else's, and when Kim heard this, she responded by putting me last on the schedule.

That meant I might not get to show my demo at all. My opportunity would turn on Scott's unpredictable schedule, and his availability could change in an instant. Sometimes he'd get a phone call from Steve and dash out with his phone pressed to his ear, never to return that day. Other times he was delayed, so we would have to fit a long slate of demos into a reduced time period, and when that happened, the last ones would be dropped. Sometimes discussing the merits of the most promising demos, which were scheduled first, took far longer than anticipated, and we simply ran out of time to look at everything. I was keen to show my keyboard, but everyone else felt the same about their own, and they all had complied with the official demo procedure.

When Scott arrived to see keyboards on demo day, everyone on the software team was gathered in the main Purple team conference room, which was called Between. Across the hall, there were two other rooms: A Rock and A Hard Place. It had been about a month since Henri made his hallway keyboard announcement, and everyone had made a serious effort, but it wasn't clear we were out of our tight spot concerning keyboards.

Scott took a chair at the long wooden table in Between, a Wallaby prototype tethered to a Mac lying on the desk. Scott picked up the Wallaby, and as he started each demo on offer in the switcher app, the programmer who created the demo stepped forward to describe how it functioned. These how-to instructions could be complicated. Some involved blue-sky interaction models, like one colleague's complex multiple-tap scheme built around a few super-big keys he could type on without looking. Others called for various orchestrations of multitouch inputs to type letters, enter punctuation, and capitalize words. Scott was game to try everything, and as always, he was upbeat and encouraging. He found something positive to say about each demo—good graphics, clever idea, interesting concept—but he was still having a difficult time. None of the keyboards offered quick and accurate typing.

As Scott tapped and swiped through demo after demo, I stood around, shuffling my feet. I checked the time. When Scott finished looking at the last keyboard in the demo switcher, he glanced over to Kim to ask what was next. I guess she forgot about my add-on demo since it wasn't integrated with the others, so she said, "Well, that's it."

"No!"

I blurted it out. It came out as more of a shout than I would have liked, but a rush of adrenaline had gotten the better of me. Scott turned to look at me. With the sound of my heart beating in my ears, I explained that I had a keyboard to show, but it would take me a moment to reconfigure the Mac connected to the Wallaby prototype. Scott pushed his chair back so I could get to the computer and launch my demo, and a few seconds later, I handed the Wallaby back to him.

He asked me how my demo worked. I told him to tap the letters he wanted to type and to ignore that there were multiple letters on each key—the software would figure out what he wanted.

Scott gave a half nod, turned his attention to the Wallaby, and as I watched over his shoulder, I saw him thumb-tap the five keys to type his name: **as zxc op rt rt**. He typed quickly, and when he looked up, he saw his name spelled correctly. He deleted a few times and tried it once more. After tap-tap-tap-tap-tap, he again saw:

Satisfied with that, he tapped a few more times:

yui as space nm yui space nm as nm qwe

He looked up and saw the complete sentence:

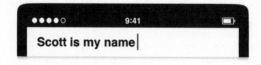

Much easier done than said. Scott turned around to me and said, "This is amazing!" Everyone else was silent for a moment, then Scott's questions started raining down.

"Why are there multiple letters on the keys?"

"How does your software know which letter I wanted?"

"How does it figure out the word I meant?"

I explained that my software checked all the combinations for all the letters he'd typed and chose the most likely word from a dictionary I created. He asked me how I put the dictionary together, how I evaluated words against each other, why I grouped the letters as I did on the big keys, and on and on. One question followed the other in rapid succession. I had spent long hours on this keyboard over the past several days and many more thinking about possible bugs and problems. I knew my software, inside and out.

After my demo, the meeting broke up, and Scott left the conference room. As usual, he didn't mill around, but other people did, and this gave them the chance to try my keyboard. They were supportive, but they clearly didn't think my keyboard was as "amazing" as Scott did. That's how it often goes with early-stage prototypes.

The final verdict on the keyboard meeting came fast, within the next day or two. Henri told us that Scott had made his decision and that we could go back to the projects we had been working on before. The keyboard emergency had passed. The Purple software engineering team could now resume our regularly scheduled programming. Except for me. Henri said that

Scott wanted me to be the DRI for keyboards. Scott didn't even bother asking me if I was willing to sign up for the job.

I had just figured out what was next.

*　*　*

There were a few more twists and turns on this keyboard project than was typical—the hallway pause, the all-hands redirection toward a single technology investigation, the dramatic demo derby—but the overall process that led up to this meeting with Scott was standard Apple.

The Purple hallway had been a swirl of activity. We shared our best ideas with each other about how to move forward from where we were. We worked hard, and we could provide some typical Silicon Valley evidence of that—we had a corner near Scott's office where we stacked our empty pizza boxes. Even so, it's not enough to look at how we arrived at a promising result on a new technology after a determined push over a few weeks and explain it by saying: We collaborated.

Exactly *how* we collaborated mattered, and for us on the Purple project, it reduced to a basic idea: We showed demos to each other. Every major feature on the iPhone started as a demo, and for a demo to be useful to us, it had to be *concrete and specific*.

We needed concrete and specific demos to guide our work, since even an unsophisticated idea is hard to discuss constructively without an artifact to illustrate it. Here's an example:

> *Think of a cute puppy. Picture one in your mind. Close your eyes if you need to. Make the image as detailed as you can. Take a moment. A cute puppy.*
>
> *Got one? I do too, and I did well. In fact, I think my puppy is cuter than yours.*

Consider the scenario. Two people have imagined two cute puppies. I assert mine is cuter. What do we do now? Do we have a *cuteness* argument? How can we? We have nothing to go on. Do I try to describe the puppy in my mind and attempt to sway you that my vision of a golden retriever puppy is superlatively cute— because *everyone knows* that golden retrievers are the cutest of all dog breeds—and therefore, my conjured mental picture is unbeatably cute. Do you try to make a sketch on a whiteboard of the puppy you're thinking of but then apologize because you're a lousy artist, so I'll just have to take your word for how cute your puppy really is in your mind? Let's say you're my manager. What do you do now . . . pull rank?

The scenario is ridiculous. There's no way to resolve this conflict. Without a concrete and specific example of a cute puppy, there's no way to make progress.

Now, I can make this easier. Here are pictures of two cute puppies.

Now we can talk about the merits of these options. I can make my case for the cuteness of the golden retriever on the left. You might favor the lovable bulldog and attempt to persuade me that the dog-smiley happy face and single flopped-over ear make it cuter. I might argue back, pointing out the extraordinarily cute way the retriever's paws are buried in the not-so-tall grass. If we weren't satisfied with these two choices, we could search the web for countless others.

The point is that concrete and specific examples make the difference between a discussion that is difficult, perhaps *impossible*, to have and one that feels like child's play.

At Apple, we built our work on this basic fact. Demos made us react, and the reactions were essential. Direct feedback on one demo provided the impetus to transform it into the next. Demos were the catalyst for creative decisions, and we found

that the sooner we started making creative decisions—whether we should have big keys with easy-to-tap targets or small keys coupled with software assistance—the more time there was to refine and improve those decisions, to backtrack if needed, to forge ahead if possible. Concrete and specific demos were the handholds and footholds that helped boost us up from the bottom of the conceptual valley so we could scale the heights of worthwhile work. Making a succession of demos was the core of the process of taking an idea from the intangible to the tangible.

Making demos is hard. It involves overcoming apprehensions about committing time and effort to an idea that you aren't sure is right. At Apple, we then had to expose that idea and demo to the scrutiny of sharp-eyed colleagues who were never afraid to level pointed criticism. The psychological hurdle only grows taller with the knowledge that most demos—almost all of them—fail in the absolute, dead-end sense of the word.

This prospect of likely failure can make it tough to sit down, focus, and make a demo at all. Getting another cup of coffee can sound better, especially if a couple colleagues are willing to go along, and then when everybody returns from the communal break, the whiteboard may beckon, and the group might veer off into a gab session.

We didn't do this on the Purple project. We rarely had brainstorming sessions. I recall only a few times in my entire Apple career when I stood around to rough out big plans at a whiteboard. Even when it did happen, as in my story from chapter 3, when we hashed out the porting strategy for our web browser project, we chatted, sketched, and came to our decisions as quickly as we could. If brainstorms run longer than an hour or so, or if there are more than a handful of people in attendance, or if they're a common occurrence, they can devolve into a form of sneaky procrastination. Whiteboard discussions feel like work, but often they're not, since it's too difficult to talk productively about ideas in the abstract. *Think of a cute puppy.*

The Purple team rarely worked without concrete and specific artifacts, and the story of the keyboard derby illustrates how. Although we had little collective experience with touchscreen software keyboards before Henri told us to start working on them, that lack of grounding didn't matter to us. Starting from our hallway meeting, we picked a point over the technological horizon and, together, we set out toward it, unsure if we were headed in exactly the right direction. It was hard to orient ourselves—the touchscreen text entry landscape didn't exist yet. Yet that's what innovation opportunities look like. The field was wide open, so, when any of us had a new concept for a keyboard, we made a demo to communicate what we were thinking. Literally, we had to *demonstrate* our idea. We couldn't get away with telling. We were required to show. We combined some inspiration, craft, taste, and decisiveness, and we shared our results. We had to work like this, because the team didn't accept anything unless it was concrete and specific, a demo showing what we meant. Then we tried out each other's demos, said what we liked and what we didn't, and offered suggestions for improvements, which led to more demos and more feedback. This virtuous collaborative cycle in the Purple hallway helped me to produce a promising keyboard demo, one the company was willing to back.

My derby winner was like a Black Slab Encounter for the Purple keyboard. It set the course for the period of work that followed, and oddly enough, the keys on my keyboard did look like little alien obelisks tipped over onto their sides.

7

QWERTY

If you've ever owned an iPhone, you know that the keyboard I presented during the demo derby does not look or work like the one that appeared on the product that shipped. What happened?

To begin with, everyone else went back to their pre-derby programming tasks, and all the responsibility for developing the keyboard, which had been shared collectively among the Purple software team for a few weeks, landed squarely in my lap.

As the new keyboard DRI, I had plenty of questions to answer. Would my derby-winning keyboard be good enough as it was? Would I be able to improve it? Would I be able to develop a dictionary that always suggested the right word? Would people like it, or at least stick with it long enough to decide if they liked it?

Finding the answers became a balancing act among craft, taste, and empathy—developing touchscreen text entry technology that was efficient, likable, and intuitive. All along, I worried that my keyboard had product-killing potential. Indeed, there was a well-known precedent in Apple's own history.

Apple once made a product that was torpedoed by its poor text entry technology—the Newton, the handheld personal digital assistant the company created in the 1990s. The Newton was groundbreaking in concept and form factor, but it was sunk by its problematic handwriting recognition.[1]

While the Newton was also hampered by its lack of connectivity, a dearth of compelling use cases, and the absence of a killer app—a program so good that people would buy the device just so they could use it—none of that matters. The substandard speed and accuracy of the Newton's stylus-based text entry drowns out all other memories of the product. The Newton stylus could have joined the Mac mouse and the iPod click wheel as a landmark in computer input methods, but it didn't.

A few people on the Purple project, including Greg Christie, had worked on the Newton, and they were all too aware of why the Apple PDA failed. To them, my keyboard seemed like a chance for history to repeat itself. Every bug or deficiency in my keyboard prompted one of them to invoke the Newton, and in the Keynote slide decks Henri periodically prepared for Scott to give him a progress update on our biggest software risks for Purple, I quickly got used to the keyboard showing up on the first slide, always near the top.

To succeed where the Newton didn't, I would need to do more than solve the next technical problem. It wouldn't merely be a matter of coding craft. The keyboard was different. None of us knew how a touchscreen keyboard was *supposed* to work. I had to constantly ask myself whether what seemed like a good solution to me was actually a good solution. I didn't know. Typing on a small sheet of glass was new.

Within a week of picking my keyboard, Scott scheduled a private demo with Phil Schiller, Apple's top marketing executive, the man who, after Steve, was most responsible for communicating to prospective customers exactly why we thought our products were great and why they should go out and buy one.

Scott didn't clue me in on the politics in play between him and Phil or why he had scheduled the demo. I imagined that Scott was eager to show off the results of the keyboard derby, which must have been a topic for discussion up at the executive level. In any case, my job was to prepare my demo so it worked as it did for the demo derby, so that's what I did.

When Scott brought Phil to the conference room, I was waiting. This was the first time I ever met Phil, and I was nervous. I set everything up as I had a few days earlier, but I had already made a couple of changes to the keyboard user interface. Scott introduced me. Phil greeted me with a quick courtesy that showed he wanted to get right down to business.

He picked up the Wallaby and tapped a few times. I didn't see what he typed. Phil asked me why I'd put more than one letter on every key. He was pleasant but direct. He seemed to think that my keyboard looked odd, that it required an explanation.

I tried to give him one. I told him about our decisions to make big keys that were easy to target and couple them with suggestions from a dictionary.

Phil wasn't satisfied, and he said so. Then that was it. I was surprised we were done so fast. The demo was over in about two minutes.

It was sobering to hear Phil's point of view. Obviously, he had none of the emotional connection I had to my keyboard. While I had been working hard on it, for Phil it was brand new, and he was indifferent to it. He expected the software to win him over, and apparently, it didn't. This mattered for two reasons. First,

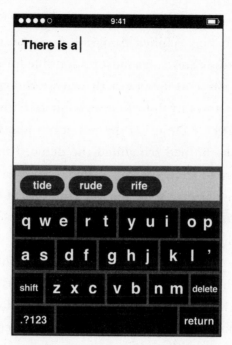

The derby-winning keyboard with some modifications to make it more full-featured. The shift and delete keys made way for a return key and a key to display numbers and punctuation.

as I said, Phil would be playing a pivotal role in pitching the Purple phone to people in the outside world once we were done developing it. Second, and perhaps more important, his reaction was just like a prospective customer evaluating a product from scratch. My keyboard would be a part of the overall impression, and Phil was confused rather than convinced.

A couple days later, Scott and I repeated the demo performance for Tony Fadell, the executive in charge of the iPod division. I had never met Tony before either, but I didn't have to know him to see how preoccupied he was. When he walked over to the conference room table with my demo on it, he barely glanced at my keyboard. He didn't ask any questions. Then he tried my software, but he couldn't have typed more than a word or two. The demo with him was even shorter than the one for Phil, and within a minute, he and Scott went off together for a private meeting, leaving me alone in the conference room to clean up the Mac, the Wallaby, and the wires connecting them.

Two demos with less-than-positive responses. Add that to my fellow derby entrants' lack of excitement, and I could tell we didn't yet have exactly the right solution. I didn't get to demo the software for Steve. Maybe Scott concluded that we weren't ready for the big time, but he never said anything specific to me about these executive demos, good or bad.

I didn't feel like I had let Scott down. There were no bad bugs during these executive demos. As I tried to interpret the feedback and decide what to do next, I thought back to the Black Slab Encounter with Safari. That breakthrough didn't represent an end; it signaled a beginning. As exciting as it was to see our web browser render the first sliver of a web page, we realized what the milestone meant. I began to look at my derby-winning design in a similar way, as if it were a successful audition rather than a sold-out performance.

I started to think about improvements, and to help me keep my keyboard goal literally in sight as I sat in my office, I measured and cut out a small piece of paper, about 2 inches wide by 1.3 inches tall, a little smaller than half the size of a credit card turned on end. I pinned up this little slip of paper on the bulletin board next to my desk. I looked at it often. This was all the screen real estate I had available for my keyboard. This was my touchscreen typing canvas. People would have to tap-tap-tap in that tiny rectangle to type, and I had to figure out how to make that happen. As I pondered that small shape and took stock of my software, I got accustomed to the idea that I might need to rethink some of the decisions that led to the derby-winning design, perhaps all of them.

Weeks went by, and I made demo after demo, trying new ideas to improve the typing experience. I added more words to the dictionary. I experimented with displaying the top word suggestion on the space bar as an extra hint that it was the word the software would enter if you typed a space. Since Richard Williamson's office was right next to mine, I often poked my head around his door, called him into my office, and invited him to pick up the Wallaby so he could try my latest ideas. He always gave specific feedback. More words in the dictionary—good. Word hint on the space bar—not so good.

This kind of collaboration was common. The programmers and designers on the Purple project were in and out of each other's offices all the time. We exchanged frequent feedback on our work, and all of us were expected to field questions on our specific area of development. If the developer of the Contacts app had a suggestion or comment about using the keyboard to type a person's first or last name into the appropriate field on a contact card, I was the one to ask about it. As it turned out, this exact task, typing people's names, proved to be a stumbling block for the derby-winning keyboard.

Consider what it would be like to type a word on a keyboard where there were multiple letters on every key. Typing a key made

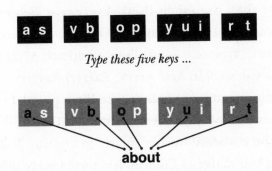

Type these five keys ...

... and the keyboard could figure out you meant to type "about."

all the letters on that key a possible choice for that position in the word. Tapping the **as** key made it just as likely you meant to type a word that began with "a" or "s." As you typed more keys and then tapped **space**, the software would offer the best word for all the keys you typed by selecting the best letter for each position.

This scheme worked well for common words, and every new word I added to the dictionary made it work even better.

Typing people's names was another matter. What if you had a friend named Teemu? Since I never added dictionary entries for popular given names for men from Finland, typing his name was impossible. My keyboard had no trouble with finding paths for ordinary English words, but the software couldn't find a path through a succession of keys for a name like Teemu, since his name wasn't in the dictionary.

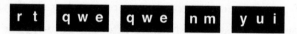

If you typed these five keys for the name "Teemu,"
you were out of luck. Since this name wasn't in the
dictionary, the keyboard couldn't match it.

The problem for uncommon words was similar. What if you wanted to type a gibberish word on purpose? This happens much more than you might think. Every year, September 19 is International Talk Like a Pirate Day.[2] On this humorous holiday, people want to type one word above all others: Arrr! Of course. But how do you spell it: Arr? Arrrr? Aarrrr? Aarrrrr? To make it easy and convenient for people to type like a pirate, I would have to add every one of these "Arrr!" permutations to the dictionary, since the keyboard wasn't "smart" in any way. It didn't have any built-in knowledge of English. It couldn't make inferences or sound things out. The keyboard could suggest a word only if the dictionary contained an exact entry for that word.

How could I help people type Finnish names and onomatopoeia? I didn't know. Could I add all the names for all the world's languages, and if I did, could I reliably differentiate between a misspelled word and an uncommon name? I doubted it. Could I anticipate every bit of humorous babble people might want to type? Fuhgettaboutit.

These problems illustrate a common product development quandary. People who love tech gadgets want new products that do cool new things. This creates the customer demand that gives product developers like me incentive to add new features. Yet none of us wants these products and features to be confusing, to lead us astray, to drive us down a software dead end and dump us there. We've all owned devices that had too many ill-considered, overlapping, and inscrutable features, making the products nearly impossible to understand or use. Apple's whole identity was bound up in not having this problem.

Over time, I came to the conclusion that designing an excellent user experience was as much about preventing negative experiences as facilitating positive ones. It couldn't be an even trade-off either. Great products make people happy almost all the time and do the opposite rarely, if at all. This worried me because, as matters stood, my derby-winning keyboard might wipe the smile off someone's face on International Talk Like a Pirate Day. On that holiday, my keyboard had to deliver on **Arrr!**, not cause people to give up in frustration, exclaiming "Argh!"

But before I could figure out how to type personal names or keyboard like a pirate, a more serious problem came up. As my teammates on the Purple project used my keyboard in their daily routine in the months following the demo derby, they found they were getting confused in the midst of the tapping through words letter by letter. Something was obstructing the customary thinking and typing process. My teammates reported how they would start to type a word but then lose track of their progress somewhere in the middle. I had no idea what the problem was or why it seemed to happen much more with my keyboard than it did on a desktop or laptop computer. When this new-found touchscreen keyboard confusion struck, the remedy was to stop, delete a partially typed word, and then retype it again from the beginning. Once it became clear to me how frequently my colleagues were doing this, I stopped fretting about typing "Teemu" and "Arrr!" so I could investigate why my teammates were getting lost. After a little study, I figured out what was going on.

The derby winner suggested only those words with the exact number of letters you'd typed. My dictionary lookup software didn't predict longer words. From today's perspective, this seems like a huge limitation, but again, we were making it up as we went along. We were in the equivalent of the touchscreen-typing Stone Age. We were making new discoveries all the time about how a touchscreen keyboard should work, and as it turned out, this stop-delete-retype problem was a significant finding about the implications of putting multiple letters on a single key.

Here's an example. I start typing the word "aluminum" but then get distracted momentarily—perhaps a colleague invites me to get a cup of coffee. Let's say I typed five letters before my attention was diverted. When I want to refocus and continue typing, I have to ask myself "Where am I? What letter comes next?" I look up to the suggestion bar, the narrow rectangle situated directly above the keyboard that displayed candidates from the dictionary, hoping for some assistance. The software offers me a word: **slimy.**

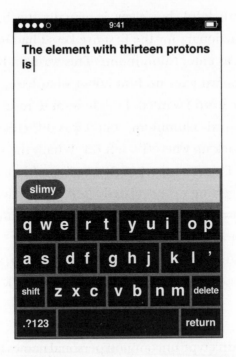

The element with thirteen protons is|

slimy

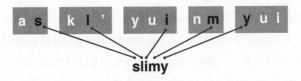

When I typed five keys, the derby-winning keyboard suggested words of five letters. If I started to type "aluminum," but then got distracted after tapping five keys, it was difficult to get started again.

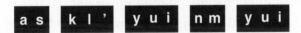
slimy

Can you think of the sixth letter in "aluminum" without counting? It's easier to delete and retype. Unfortunately, the best five-letter word for these letters is "slimy."

This is unhelpful, but **slimy** is actually the best five-letter word in the dictionary for the first five keys I had to type on the derby winner to enter "aluminum." This wasn't a bug. Not only that, the keyboard gave no hint about what letter I should tap next to get the word I wanted. I might want to resume my typing to finish the word "aluminum," but it was difficult to figure out how to pick back up where I'd left off. What's the sixth letter of "aluminum"? This is a surprisingly tough question, and with the keyboard suggesting an unrelated word, it was easier to delete the partial word and start again. I wanted "aluminum," but I got **slimy**. Technological tragicomedy.

There was no obvious solution to this problem, and with this latest difficulty, the issues with the derby-winning keyboard were piling up:

- We couldn't type uncommon personal names like "Teemu."
- We couldn't type uncommon words like "Arrr!"
- We were getting lost while typing—the "Where am I?" problem.

Every day, my teammates were updating to the latest keyboard software, loading it onto their Wallaby prototype devices, and trying it out. There's a common high-tech term for a daily regimen of using and evaluating your own product while you're trying to develop it: *dogfooding.* I never liked this term myself, and it didn't appeal to Apple sensibilities either. Pet food isn't typically thought of as a pinnacle of product development. On the Purple hallway, we were trying to make excellent products for people, and while we sometimes said "dogfooding" inside Apple, more often, and more officially, we began to say "living on" to describe the day-to-day routine of living on our in-progress software like it was a real product.

The living-on experience with my derby-winning keyboard was a mixed bag. It was working well enough for typing messages and emails using common words, but the drawbacks were too big to ignore, and on my own, I was struggling to find fixes for the problems on my list.

In early 2006, about three months after the keyboard derby, a dozen of us met in the Between conference room to review our overall progress with Scott Forstall and several programmers and managers. Greg Christie was there as well, along with a few designers from his HI team. Scott was trying some typical living-on experiences with the Purple software, Wallaby in hand, and he was typing. We weren't focused on the keyboard specifically, but then Scott got lost in the middle of typing a medium-length word: **national**.

After tapping four keys, **nm as rt yui**, Scott looked up and saw **Mary** in the suggestion bar, and he got a little thrown off, but he recovered enough to type the next key, **op**. But when he peeked at the suggestion bar again, he saw **Mario**. Now he was totally lost. He had no idea what to type next. Scott ran smack into the "Where am I?" problem. He told me how he felt the only way to wind up with the word he wanted was to stop, delete, and retype. Others chimed in, and of course, I had already heard this kind of feedback. Now that we were together, we started digging into the problem as a group.

I stepped up to the whiteboard and drew diagrams that showed how trying to type the word "national" might produce suggestions of **Mary** and **Mario** in the midst of typing. I explained why that made sense. Before long I was describing the two other main problems with the derby-winning design. I mentioned that, while **Mary** and **Mario** were the unwanted distractions on the way to typing "national," typing a less common name, like "Teemu," could be impossible since the name wasn't in the dictionary. I gave my opinion that we would never be able to add dictionary entries for all the names for all the people of the world. I also went over the difficulty of typing "Arrr!" and how we would never be able to add dictionary entries for all the reasonably sensible gibberish people might want to type.

After describing these problems, I backed up a bit to review the four basic concepts of the derby-winning keyboard:

1. Big keys with multiple letters per key
2. A QWERTY arrangement
3. Every gesture was a tap
4. A dictionary provided active assistance

I suggested that there was something not quite right about these principles as a summed total. As we got more experience living on a keyboard based on these ideas, we kept tripping over ourselves as we tried to type. The derby winner was good at typing common short words but ran into trouble with people's names, uncommon words, and long words. Something had to be done, but I didn't know what.

By now I had been up at the whiteboard for about ten or fifteen minutes, and I had totally derailed the demo. This meeting wasn't supposed to be a keyboard deep-dive session, but it was now. Marker in hand, I sketched more big keys with multiple letters on them, more examples of letter combinations, and more diagrams of the most sensible word paths through typical sets of typed keys. I really didn't know what else to do, so I just spilled everything I knew about the problems with the keyboard as best I could.

Greg Christie broke the logjam. He decided that he'd seen enough of my drawings. He had heard enough of my explanations.

He wanted to return to the other demos we had been reviewing. To him, the design solution was simple. So he hollered at me, much like a New Yorker trying to get the attention of a roving hotdog vendor at a crowded baseball game, "Aww . . . come on, Ken! Can't you just put one letter on every key?"

Greg got my attention all right, and it wasn't just his brusque manner. Since I grew up in the New York area myself, I could look past his direct East Coast communication style more easily than some of my teammates. Greg never sugarcoated his comments. If he thought a feature was no good, he told you. But when Greg gave feedback, I always listened for a hint of exasperation, as if what he was saying were obvious. If he had that tetchy tinge in his voice, it meant he was confident. I was still standing at the whiteboard with marker in hand when Greg spoke up, and it sounded to me like he was awfully sure of himself.

I thought quickly about what he'd said. He wanted me to change the keyboard to a design that had one letter on every key. I looked back at my sketches of big keys with multiple letters on them. I got an idea. I told Greg, "Yeah, maybe there's something I can do."

When I thought more after the demo broke up, Greg's reasoning became clear to me. As he listened to me describe the four basics of my derby-winning keyboard—big keys with multiple letters per key, QWERTY arrangement, tap gestures, dictionary assistance—Greg realized the weak link in the chain was the first of them. He zeroed in on having multiple letters per key. He thought that was the design decision holding back progress. That was the root problem. His proposal was to change back to a small-key design with only one letter on each key. Of course, it was easy enough for Greg to say that, once he had the insight to think it, but I doubt he had the slightest idea how it might be accomplished in software.

But with the keyboard development experience I'd accumulated thus far, maybe I did. Within a day or two, I had a plan and some code to back it up. Just as Greg had suggested, I went back to small keys with just one letter per key. I had been working for months on the QWERTY layout, tap to type, and the word-matching dictionary. With these three technologies combined, I had a better shot at making smaller keys work.

The other difference came from the idea I had while standing at the whiteboard in the conference room. On a conceptual level, it was about designing the keyboard as a means for people to communicate their intent to the device and structuring the software so it could understand that intent. This is an important concept for touchscreen user interfaces, and I'll return to discuss this notion—interpreting what people mean given what they do—more fully in the next chapter. To capitalize on Greg's single-letter-per-key suggestion, I got the idea that the person typing and the autocorrection code didn't have to see the keyboard the same way. On the derby-winning keyboard, they did—the groupings of multiple letters were fixed both for the typist and for the software. For example, the letters **QWE** were always together. In my new, Greg-inspired layout, each letter appeared by itself on a key but was given a new set of neighbors as far as the autocorrection code was concerned. For example, the letter **F** was no longer locked in a **DF** set. For the person typing, there was a clearly defined **F** key, but the autocorrection code saw **F** as part of a custom group, **FDGRTC**, with **F** in the center and all its neighbors to the left and right, above and below. The keys actually got bigger from the autocorrection standpoint, even though visually they appeared smaller to the typist.

Once I banished the hardwired key groupings, the design choice Phil Schiller didn't like, I had something that looked more like a standard QWERTY keyboard.

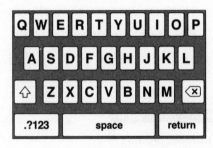 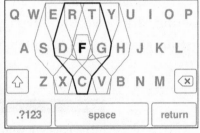

*For the typist, all the keys shrank in size, as compared to
the derby-winning keyboard, as shown on the left. The
autocorrection software saw the F key as much larger, as shown
on the right, since typing in the area of D, G, R, T, or C might
result in autocorrection choosing an F, but it also might result
in choosing one of those other letters. All keys were similarly
enlarged from the autocorrection point of view, and the
keys neighboring F are shown to illustrate the overlaps.
It was up to the autocorrection code to figure out which
letters on these enlarged keys you really meant.*

This was another important step in the development of the
keyboard and the solution to my lingering problems. Single-letter keys provided the escape hatch for typing names and uncommon words. Since you could target an individual letter, you could
type whatever word you wanted. Even if you needed to be extra
careful, you could slow down your typing and give extra attention to the keys as they popped up.* If you looked at the pop-
ups and always hit the right key, you could type anything, even
words that weren't in the dictionary. Even better, changing over
to single-letter keys definitively solved the "Where am I?" problem. Since I always displayed the specific sequence of keys you

---

*I don't recall who came up with the idea first for touchscreen typing, but
we all recognized the strength of the pop-up concept once we saw it. I developed my own version around this time with considerable help from Bas
Ording. His deft touch always made everything better.

actually tapped, you could always look up and find your place. Getting distracted while typing "aluminum" no longer meant getting **slimy**.

The new single-key QWERTY design provided the definitive solution to the "Where am I?" problem.

The single-letter QWERTY keyboard really was better. Greg Christie was right. Within a few days after making this change, I no longer had a pile of problems with no solutions in sight. Now you could type people's names. You could type like a pirate. You wouldn't get lost in the middle of words.

Even so, solving these lingering problems revealed the next issue, a subtle behavior about the new QWERTY keyboard and the space bar. From the start of my investigations into providing active dictionary assistance, I aimed my user interface and technical designs at helping people type individual words. Tapping the space bar was an important trigger.

On the derby-winning keyboard, when you tapped **space**, the software picked the best word corresponding to the keys typed. Since every key represented multiple letters, there was no way to specifically indicate which letter you wanted. The software and dictionary had to choose the word for you when you tapped **space**.

When I switched away from this automatic-word-choosing on the Greg-inspired, single-letter QWERTY keyboard, tapping **space** now entered the exact characters you typed, the ones you saw pop up as you tapped. Dictionary suggestions continued to be visible in the suggestion bar, and I placed the best dictionary suggestion in the left position. Your exact typing appeared in the right position. However, getting dictionary assistance required tapping the word bubble in the suggestion bar rather than tapping **space**. You needed to pause at the end of typing a word, look up at the letters you had actually typed, tap **space** if you had typed accurately, or tap a bubble to change to a software suggestion. This change in interaction model seemed correct, like I was returning full control to the typist. If you wanted to type "Arrr!," you could, simply and directly. That was the whole idea of putting one letter on every key. Tapping **space** gave you the letters you typed.

Since everyone on the Purple development team was living on my new QWERTY keyboard every day, the feedback came back to me loud and clear. It was too hard to build up typing speed. The keys were too small, key-by-key accuracy was too low, and entering text involved too much looking in the suggestion bar. Those suggestion bar bubbles were like speed bumps.

As before, I continued to talk with Richard Williamson every day about the keyboard, and we started discussing eliminating these speed bumps. First of all, both of us thought the dictionary suggestions were getting noticeably better. A common typing pattern became: type a word, tap the left suggestion bar bubble to get the top dictionary suggestion, type a word, tap the left suggestion bar bubble. Again, and again, and again. We thought that, perhaps, we should reintroduce the behavior where tapping the space bar was a signal for the software to make a choice. What if the keyboard automatically entered the top dictionary suggestion when you hit the space bar, making it more like the derby-winning keyboard? This meant you might need to tap a bubble in the suggestion bar to get your exact typing if it was different from the word the dictionary software suggested, but as Richard and I chatted about this idea, we thought that might be all right, since you would need to resort to tapping a bubble only for "Arrr!" and other uncommon words. We also expressed some apprehension that the keyboard would routinely change your typing out from under you—the word you got after tapping **space** might not correspond to the exact keys you had hit. Would this be a problem? We didn't know, but we thought it might be the solution to the speed bump problem. Richard suggested I try it, and just for kicks, I agreed.

He left my office, I wrote some code, and in about a half hour, I had a new demo of the QWERTY keyboard, one that automatically picked the best dictionary word suggestion when you tapped **space**.

I called Richard back into my office. He picked up the Wallaby from my desk. He was determined to find out if the suggestion bar speed bumps were really gone. He put his head down and started jabbing quickly at the touchscreen. He thumb-typed as fast as he could. He typed, typed, typed. He never paused or stopped to look up. He trusted the software. When he was done typing his long sentence, he typed a period. Then he looked up at the text to see how he did.

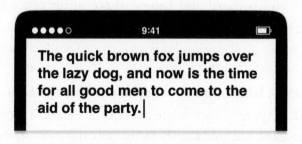

Just as he intended. Richard did a slapstick-style double take. He looked at the screen again and examined each word closely to make sure he actually saw the flawless typing he thought he was seeing. He showed me the display. We looked at each other and burst out laughing. We couldn't believe how well the dictionary figured out everything. Richard just typed far more quickly than anybody had ever typed anything on a Wallaby.

Wait . . . wait . . . just a second. We had a moment of doubt. Was this real? Did Richard just type with super accuracy?

No. I had a log file on the Mac tethered to the Wallaby, and it showed that Richard's actual typing was horribly imprecise, a complete mess, like a drunkard hilariously failing a spelling sobriety test:

Tge quixk brpwm foz jimprd ivrr rhe kazy . . .

It didn't matter. Even though Richard's actual keyboarding was riddled with errors, it was close enough to what he wanted that the software could fix all his mistakes. Junky key presses produced perfect typing—the opposite of the *garbage in, garbage out* way computers were supposed to work. We looked back down at the keyboard again, then up to each other again. We couldn't believe it. Touchscreen keyboard autocorrection was born in that moment, and Richard and I stood there in my office together, giggling like little kids.

* * *

The Black Slab Encounter was one of only two *Eureka!* moments I ever had at Apple. This was the other one. I made a lot of demos over the years, but this Giggly Demo was the best. Richard's reaction, the joyful laughter, the giddiness both of us felt in that moment of discovery about a new piece of software, the potential that always-on autocorrection might be a giant step in the right direction. It was an easy decision to make this keyboard change permanent.

Months later, after we announced our smartphone to the public but before we shipped the first devices to customers, those of us on the software team started carrying around late-stage prototypes as our daily use phones. One day I got a visit from Nitin Ganatra, the other Purple software manager reporting to Henri. He was Richard's peer, responsible for apps like SpringBoard and Mail. Nitin stopped by my office to ask me some workaday question, nothing momentous, and when he walked in, he was munching on a candy bar. We talked about this or that for a minute, then the conversation turned to typing. He took his phone out of his pocket. Holding the prototype hardware in his left hand, Nitin brought up the then-current version of my keyboard, a direct descendant of the Giggly Demo code. He started typing. He didn't bother to put down his candy bar, and he poked at my updated autocorrection code using only the middle finger of his right hand and his left thumb. The peeled-back snack wrapper in his right hand crinkled as he typed. Then he leaned the screen toward me so I could see his perfect keyboarding. I forget what he typed, but I remember his approving nod.

As we developed software products at Apple, programming and design details were foremost in our minds. We moved past each prototype quickly and started making the next one. This visit from Nitin was different. His correct typing, candy bar in hand, was a moment to stop and think. Maybe this keyboard someday might fit neatly and unobtrusively into people's everyday lives. Maybe people wouldn't need to stop everything else they were doing to use this gadget.

Would that really be true? Would full-time autocorrection contribute to that? Was the keyboard finally on the right track?

And what about that QWERTY key layout? Was that the right choice? You may know that QWERTY is an acronym whose constituent letters come from the top row displayed on the keyboards for many Latin scripts, and it wasn't a forgone conclusion we would wind up with this most popular of letter layouts for our smartphone.[3] As I've shown, we came around to QWERTY fairly late in the progression of prototypes. We considered many other options first. Yet, in the end, we came back around to the most familiar keyboard design.

One legend swirls more persistently around the QWERTY design than all others: how its inventor developed the arrangement to slow down typists. This is correct, as far as it goes, but it focuses on the wrong thing. Given the limits of nineteenth-century technology and the need for a complex scheme to actuate a series of metallic keys to strike a page, a major problem was developing a system where the keys didn't jam. The time it took to clear key jams was the real bane of speedy typists, so QWERTY was an excellent compromise between an efficient key arrangement for people's fingers and the need for a typing apparatus to whirl and clack. The QWERTY layout actually helped people type faster.[4]

Naturally, our Purple keyboard was software, so we were free from all such mechanical requirements, as well as from form factor and tactile conventions. We could have chosen any key arrangement we wanted for Purple, and perhaps we missed a golden opportunity at the advent of touchscreen typing. We could have banished QWERTY forever. Yet this assumes QWERTY is bad. It isn't, and the reasons have to do with how taste and empathy combine with craft to make a technology like a software keyboard.

In the introduction to this book, I described empathy as *trying to see the world from other people's perspectives and creating work that fits into their lives and adapts to their needs.* Empathy is a crucial part of making great products. The living-on experiences with the derby-winning keyboard showed several breakdowns in empathy, where the person felt at odds with software attempting to provide assistance. Even before we realized these detailed typing problems existed, there was the initial visual impression of the keyboard. As Phil did in my demo with him, people reacted to the appearance of the keyboard. Its look communicated what the keyboard was and what it did. At Apple, we sought to be as empathetic as possible in both the initial and the ongoing experiences with a product, but we realized we couldn't try everything during our design and development phase. We needed to whittle down the unbounded possibilities for how a product might look and behave, and to do this, we used our design and technological taste.

This just raises the next question: What is good taste? I have my own opinion, which I'll share shortly, but I also realize I'm not the first to consider the topic. Immanuel Kant himself wrote at length about taste, yet his *Critique of Judgement* isn't exactly a handbook for product design.[5] If one of my colleagues had questioned the use of the QWERTY layout for the Purple keyboard as a matter of taste, it wouldn't have done much good to quote the great German philosopher: "The judgement of taste itself does not *postulate* the agreement of everyone (for that can only be done by a logically universal judgement because it can adduce reasons); it only *imputes* this agreement to every one, as a case of the rule in respect of which it expects, not confirmation by concepts, but assent from others."[6]

I don't mean to suggest that Kant isn't worth studying. Of course he is. Yet when it comes to making products, philosophical discourse is the wrong tool for the job when practical decisions are needed. It would be similar to a carpenter pausing to ponder the finer points of materials science, quantum theory, and the origins of the universe—fingers pressed to forehead in a moment of deep reflection—before choosing the right hammer to drive nails. Working that way isn't smart. As a creative and technical practitioner, I couldn't open myself to an infinite regress of ideas at every step of accomplishing a task. It's important to keep making progress and to keep sight of priorities. That doesn't give product designers the license to ignore philosophy. Rather, in my case, I recognized I'm not a philosopher myself; I'm closer to a carpenter. As a maker of products, I always turned less to the theoretical and more to the applied.

I have my own definition of *taste*, and while it isn't as profound as Kant's, it's a useful tool, like a carpenter's hammer. Taste is *developing a refined sense of judgment and finding the balance that produces a pleasing and integrated whole.*

Each of these points about taste warrants some discussion. I'll look at them in order, viewing each through the lens of empathy, and I'll use the QWERTY keyboard as the main example.

First, there's developing judgment. We all know what it's like to have a literal knee-jerk reaction and the similar figurative feeling we have when we instantly like or don't like something. I like perfectly ripe strawberries, and while this response certainly satisfies one definition for "taste," I can't say much about my preference beyond enjoying the sensation of sweetness. A lack of specific thoughts isn't a big deal when picking fruit to put on top of breakfast cereal, but such gaps are an issue in creative work. Persist too long in making choices without justifying them, and an entire creative effort might wander aimlessly. The results might be the sum of wishy-washy half decisions.

Developing the judgment to avoid this pitfall centers on the *refined-like response*, evaluating in an active way and finding the self-confidence to form opinions with your gut you can also justify with your head. It's not always easy to come to grips with objects or ideas and think about them until it's possible to express why you like them or not, yet taking part in a healthy and productive creative process requires such reflective engagement.

Building trust in a personal refined-like response takes time and practice. It also requires a measuring stick. Studying great work from the past provides the means of comparison and contrast and lets us tap into the collective creativity of previous generations. The past is a source of the timeless and enduring. This is where Kant returns to the discussion, and this notion suggests how his philosophy might figure into creative work. I can use Kant, but only if I know about him, and only to the extent that I've internalized what he said and what it means to me. The same goes for the whole scope of creative achievement, from the paintings of Frida Kahlo, the blues music of the Reverend Gary Davis, the theories of Charles Darwin, the philosophy of Lao Tzu, the software optimization ideas of Donald Knuth, or the beliefs and practices of the ancient Greek visitors to the Delphic Oracle. When I study the past, I make a point of deciding what I like, and sometimes this built-up catalog of refined-like responses about past works finds a suitable outlet and a natural expression in my present-day work.

What does this have to do with QWERTY? This keyboard arrangement is also a part of our cultural inheritance, even if it's not as high-minded as Kant's philosophical musings on taste. Most important, the long-standing popularity of QWERTY means that people are familiar with it. Consider the Giggly Demo with Richard. Since he knew where all the letters were on a QWERTY keyboard, he could come into my office, pick up the Wallaby, and pound out the words he wanted without thinking about it. QWERTY tapped into decades of Richard's muscle memory. He instinctively knew how to type. His QWERTY mental map translated very well from ten-finger movements on a full-sized keyboard to thumb-typing on a touchscreen. From my perspective as a product designer, I couldn't have offered Richard anything else that made better use of the knowledge I could expect him to have, based on our shared cultural experience. From his perspective as a user, no other key arrangement would have been so easy to use right away.

This set of facts formed a chain linking likability with empathy. It began with Richard's nearly automatic response to QWERTY and soon transitioned into a happy and productive text entry experience for him. Both of us laughed over it, and this makes a point. The refined-like response doesn't need to be stuffy or aspire to pretentious connoisseurship, but it does need to be detailed and justifiable. In the immediate aftermath of the Giggly Demo, there was no doubt about exactly *why* Richard and I liked what had happened. We could have described our thoughts and feelings quite clearly. The same goes for the candy bar case with Nitin.

Going beyond the refined-like response leads me to my second aspect of taste: finding balance. The development of the touchscreen keyboard is a story of searching for an equilibrium, of making the correct trade-offs. We eventually chose a single-letter QWERTY layout over my derby-winning design, but before we did, my derby-winning keyboard was a response to trying to type on too-small single-letter keys. Putting multiple letters on every key was an attempt to give away some of the familiarity with how keyboards typically look and work to get what we perceived would be improved ease of use with simpler-to-tap keys. We initially thought we liked this choice, but once we got some experience with the derby-winning multiletter key design, Greg Christie's "Aww . . . come on, Ken!" exclamation was a decisive statement that multiletter keys were a failure. Greg believed the big keys weren't contributing as much as they were detracting. Greg felt this, thought it, and then he pronounced the derby-winning keyboard unlikable and off balance, and this led directly to the return of single-letter keys and a more traditional QWERTY layout.

This is an example of how the attempt to find balance often connects my other two aspects of taste. On one side, the refined-like response is often a local determination made either early in a design process or at the specific moment of a demo. It often takes the form of "I like this animation since it helps to direct the user's attention appropriately," or "I don't like this color scheme because it fails to provide adequate contrast between these dissimilar elements," or "I like multiletter keys because they are easier to tap." Once these granular decisions are made and are incorporated into a larger system, they no longer stand alone. The small-scale justifications must contribute to a scheme larger than themselves. The design responsibility expands to balancing the many individual refined-like responses against the other side of the taste equation, the attempt to create a pleasing and integrated whole.

Before I discuss this third aspect of taste, I want to mention one characteristic that may seem to be missing from my overall notion of taste—a concern for *beauty*. My omission of beauty is not a mistake. Making software and products appear beautiful, in the sense of being visually attractive, only goes so far. Steve Jobs once said, "Design is how it works." In fact, this is my favorite thing I ever heard him say, and in the context he provided around this statement when he originally made this claim, as part of a 2003 *New York Times* interview discussing the iPod, Steve drove his point home:

> Most people make the mistake of thinking design is what it [a product] looks like. People think it's this veneer—that the designers are handed this box and told, "Make it look good!" That's not what we think design is. It's not just what it looks like and feels like. Design is how it works.[7]

His message is clear, and I agree with it. Shallow beauty in products doesn't serve people. Product design should strive for a depth, for a beauty rooted in what a product does, not merely in how it looks and feels. Form should follow function, even though this might seem like a strange notion for pixels on a screen, but it's not if you believe the appearance of a product should tell you what it is and how to use it. Objects should explain themselves.

It's impossible to overstate how much this matters, and to illustrate, I'll draw a comparison. Near the beginning of *Atoms in Motion*, Richard Feynman's first lecture introducing his two-year introductory course on physics, this famous scientist, Nobel laureate, and free-thinker extraordinaire offers his idea about the importance of atoms:

If, in some cataclysm, all of scientific knowledge were to be destroyed, and only one sentence passed on to the next generations of creatures, what statement would contain the most information in the fewest words? I believe it is the *atomic hypothesis* . . . that *all things are made of atoms* . . . In that one sentence, you will see, there is an enormous amount of information about the world, if just a little imagination and thinking are applied.[8]

In similar fashion, all my experience tells me there's a fundamental notion about practical inventions, about making a product, and if I had to choose one sentence to pass on through the Feynman void to those who come after us, it would be this: Design is how it works.

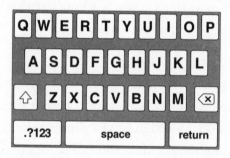

QWERTY explains itself. It unequivocally says "keyboard," but is it a design that works?

As a product development organization, we accepted this as our credo, so it was logical that our attention to creating designs that work looped back around to inform our refined-like responses, the way we tried to find balance, and our effort to create a pleasing and integrated whole. The added benefit is that this entire cycle removed the arbitrariness from taste. It gave taste a purpose, a rationale beyond self-indulgence, an empathetic end.

So, is the QWERTY keyboard a pleasing and integrated whole? Is it well balanced and justifiably likable? Is it a design that works? The intervening years have provided the answer. The autocorrecting QWERTY keyboard did not sink the iPhone as a product, as did the disappointing handwriting recognition on the Newton. The opposite happened. Two-thumb typing on a touchscreen is now normal. It's the default for mobile devices.

Even so, popularity doesn't equal excellence. A better justification is that people can type on a smartphone QWERTY keyboard without thinking about it. The keyboard can melt away, it can recede, and when it does, it leaves a space for what people really care about. A properly judged mixture of taste and empathy is the secret formula for making products that are intuitive, easy to use, and easy to live with.

One of my favorite things is watching people at the end of airline flights, soon after the landing, as the plane taxis up to the gate. When the flight attendant announces over the intercom that everyone can turn their phones on, what do many people do next? They open a messaging app and type a short note to a companion, a friend, a loved one. They say, "Just landed," or "On the ground. See you soon." These countless trivial but touching human moments are enabled by technology and made possible, in some small part, by a QWERTY keyboard.

* * *

Forgive me for jumping ahead in the story. It's time to return to the immediate aftermath of the decision to turn on full-time autocorrection. The Giggly Demo with Richard had shown the promise of an improved approach to touchscreen typing, but such glimpses of potential are not the same as a finished product. In a development process like the one for the Purple touchscreen keyboard, progress is rarely steady or constant. The demo with Richard was balanced out by less encouraging experiences. By switching to always-on autocorrection, the keyboard went into a new phase of growing pains, and in this sometimes-awkward stage, I opened up my keyboard to a new round of comparisons to Newton handwriting recognition. Right away, one such comparison was comical in more than one sense of the word.

8

Convergence

Convergence was the term we used to describe the final phase of making an Apple product, after the features had been locked down and the programming and design teams spent the last three or four months fixing bugs and polishing details. Entering a convergence period was the moment we had a clear picture in our minds about how we wanted our finished software to work. It also meant that the hardest part was over—we had been largely successful in navigating the course from idea to product.

I wasn't there yet with the keyboard. While convergence feels like a steady march to a known destination, the days around the discovery of always-on autocorrection felt more like driving a car on a highway without any signs telling which exit to take. We were still around nine months away from the convergence period for Purple, and I was busy tuning the keyboard layouts, improving the autocorrection algorithms, updating the dictionary with new words, speeding up the software, dealing with the small-scale successes and setbacks, and addressing feedback from the previous demo while preparing for the next one. I tried to keep my development moving forward, but I was never completely sure if the route I was on was the right one.

Then, whoa! A nasty autocorrection surprise sent me careening off a virtual cliff during a demo.

A few days after the Giggly Demo, when Richard first experienced the unanticipated typing accuracy possible with always-on autocorrection, I joined Henri Lamiraux in his office to give Scott Forstall a chance to try the software for himself. I set up my demo, a Wallaby tethered to a Mac, on a side table next to Henri's desk. Scott came in, sat down, picked up the Wallaby, and typed a little. I hovered over his shoulder as he tapped out his first few words. He was impressed. So far, so good. I used this opportunity to give Scott my pitch in favor of full-time autocorrection. I told him this would be how we'd deliver a great typing experience for Purple, how it would be the solution for all the problems that had plagued the derby-winning keyboard, and how it would steer us clear of the Newton's reputation for subpar text entry.

The Doonesbury strip that summed up the Newton handwriting recognition experience.

As Scott listened, he picked up on my Newton reference, and he decided to have some fun, channeling an iconic Doonesbury cartoon.

He grabbed the Wallaby and started typing, grinning as he tapped away, and when he looked up to see how my new keyboard code had done, his smile turned to laughter. When I saw the screen, I didn't think it was so funny.

I was well versed in Newton lore. I knew exactly what Scott meant to type. He wanted **egg freckles**, but that's not what he got. My keyboard botched it.

Scott thought this was hilarious, but he soon turned serious. He said my new software looked promising, but he needed to know that I could make it more consistent. He asked me if I could preserve the useful autocorrections but banish the ridiculous ones, the sort that might evoke the faulty handwriting recognition of the Newton.

I didn't know, and I said so. My confidence had been shaken by this unintentionally amusing demo, and despite my belief in my pitch about the potential of always-on autocorrection, I couldn't say how often my keyboard code might miscue. I suggested that I should start by finding out what went wrong in this particular case, and I left Henri's office shaking my head in frustration. The most embarrassing demos always seemed to happen when I showed my work to Scott.

I soon discovered the problem. Scott couldn't type "egg freckles" because two dictionary errors had compounded one another. The first was a bug in the metadata I assigned to every word in the dictionary, something I called the *usage frequency value*. This was a measure of the popularity of a word in normal text. For full-time autocorrection to work well, the code had to help people type all the most common words in English: the, and, have, from, will, and so on. The software had to know which words were more popular than others—for example, that it's more likely for people to type "good" than "goof." Hence, "good" had a higher usage frequency value than "goof." The word "the" had the highest value of all, since it's the most common word in the language. As the dictionary editor, it was my job to slot every word into a usage frequency value spectrum and give more popular words higher values than those used less often. The keyboard also had to help with everyday words like "egg," one of the top few thousand in English (right up there with "bacon"). Indeed, Scott should have gotten help typing "egg," and he would have, but for one problem: The usage frequency value for "egg" was mistakenly low, so low that the value for the relatively rare word "eff"—the spelled-out first letter of a not-nice word—was higher. This was a simple glitch in my dictionary data, and finding this bad usage frequency value was the end of the investigative trail. I sighed, fixed up the value for "egg," and muttered "eff" a few times under my breath as I did it.

What about "freckles"? It wasn't in the dictionary at all. I can't explain it. Since the keyboard saw "freckles" and couldn't find a matching dictionary entry, my code didn't think "freckles" was an English word. So, the autocorrection code swapped Scott's typing to a word that was in the dictionary: grackle, the common North American bird, *Quiscalus quiscula*.

Was there a deep lesson to learn from this "eff grackles" demo? At that point, I wasn't sure. Bad demos like this could be fixed and improved, but this incident gave everyone pause, including me. As promising as it seemed, we wondered whether keyboard autocorrection would ever be reliable enough to ship in a product and whether the sum of all the small fixes I might make would ever equal something greater.

Here's the rub. My autocorrection software had to get good at selecting between two options: switching your typing to the word that seemed most likely given your taps—what you might have meant—or keeping the exact succession of letters you tapped and saw pop up in the user interface—what you actually did. The keyboard had to make a *what you meant versus what you did* choice whenever you tapped the space bar at the end of a word. I had to teach autocorrection to make this choice well. At the same time, I had to avoid the bizarre results that might make people mistrust the software, since that might lead them to doubt their ability to type text on the touchscreen keyboard and perhaps might cause them to avoid buying our smartphone altogether—just like what happened with the Newton.

As I thought about the what-you-meant-versus-what-you-did question for the keyboard, I had two issues. The first was raising the quality of the dictionary—I needed better data. The second was making full use of all the touch input and language information I had available—I needed better algorithms. I focused on better data and better algorithms as separate tasks, hoping that the distinct threads of improvement would wind together in the end, resulting in a keyboard that accurately matched the words people intended to type while avoiding comical errors.

The "eff grackles" demo highlighted the importance of having good-quality data. There was nothing wrong with my algorithms in that session with Scott. The fault was with the dictionary. To fix this, I had to make sure everyday words like "egg" had proper usage frequencies, and I had to carefully adjust the values of similarly spelled words, especially those words with letters that are close to each other on the QWERTY keyboard, like "tune" and "time." Since missing words like "freckles" could lead to absurd mistakes, I also reviewed the dictionary for its coverage of the most common several thousand English words.

As everyone on the Purple hallway used the software day in and day out, we made surprising discoveries about what the autocorrection dictionary should contain. We found we had to add a complete collection of hate speech to the dictionary and explicitly mark those words to prevent the software from ever offering them as autocorrections—imagine trying to type "nugget" but narrowly mistyping the first vowel or the last consonant. We didn't want to offer racial epithets as a "helpful" aid, and we resolved that we would never provide software assistance for attempts to slur or demean.

My Purple teammates also let me know about the words they thought were missing from the dictionary. Over time, I decided many different data sets merited inclusion: sports team and stadium names, city names, product names, chat slang, abbreviations, and more. The autocorrection dictionary was less an academic linguistics exercise and more a catalog of contemporary life. My Purple colleagues wanted to type the words that came up in their typical day, in their typical speech, and in their typical texting taunts of friends while watching ballgames on TV:

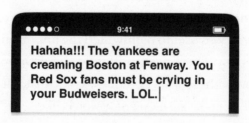

Making the autocorrection dictionary was an easy-to-understand task in theory, even though it was difficult to perform in practice. It's true that I had never engineered a large data set like this before in my career, but the concept was free of mystery. Good dictionaries are built one word at a time. This had a familiar ring to it. It was much like filling in all the cross-references during the early days of building Safari. Like the long slog of placating the compiler as it repeatedly reported errors about missing cross-references, the hard part of making a dictionary was the sheer size of the task. Yet heading toward the finish line was straightforward. Just keep tuning usage frequency values. Just keep adding words. Just keep going.

Developing the algorithms for autocorrection was different. At the kick-off of the keyboard derby, I had no idea how to make useful algorithms to assist people with text entry. Even when I had progressed through to the single-letter QWERTY keyboard layout, my autocorrection code was still extremely simple. It worked something like the tumblers on a bike lock.

If you meant to type the word "cold" but typed **colf** instead, you could imagine how spinning the fourth tumbler to a different letter would produce the desired word. This is a basic concept behind autocorrection, finding the best combination of letters given the taps from a typist, the keys that popped up, and considering the letters in the neighborhood of the popped-up key. Since the letter **D** is close to **F** on the QWERTY keyboard, the code could autocorrect from **colf** to **cold**.

The algorithm created an arrangement of tumblers corresponding to the keys you typed and the letters close to the keys you typed. Then the code whizzed through every possible combination of letters to see if any was a word. Of course, multiple words could be possible for most key sequences, and this is where

the usage frequency value in the dictionary data came into play. The algorithm worked like this:

- Arrange typed letters in a set of tumblers with their neighboring letters.
- Spin the tumblers to check every letter combination.
- Note the dictionary words found by spinning the tumblers.
- Suggest the found word with the highest usage frequency value.

I originally developed this algorithm for my derby winner, and it performed well when the keyboard had multiple letters per key. It also was a good solution when all of us on the Purple team were novices with touchscreen typing. Months later, when the single-letter QWERTY keyboard layout replaced the derby-winning design, and everyone started making more typing errors per word since the keys were so much smaller, the simple tumbler approach to autocorrection was no longer sufficient. It could reliably handle one misplaced letter in a common word, as in my **colf** to **cold** example, but it was less good at figuring out what you meant when you typed something like **vild**—was the intended word "cold," "bold," or "vile"? I didn't have a good idea for how to answer that question, so I didn't have a good idea for improving the bike lock tumbler code I had. I went looking for help.

Asking for assistance presented a problem of a different sort. I found out the names of some people at Apple who had experience building dictionaries and creating algorithms for text entry, but they weren't disclosed on the Purple project, and there was no way to get them clued in on the big smartphone secret. Back in these times, Steve Jobs himself was still playing some role in who got to sign the Purple NDA, and there was no formal system to request disclosures for new people. For good or for bad, that's not how the Purple project rolled. So, I wound up in the odd situation where I got approval to ask for help, as long as I didn't tell the people I was asking exactly why I was asking or what I planned to do with their answers.

This didn't present as big a roadblock as it could have. The Apple text experts I spoke to didn't seem overly distracted by my need for cloak-and-dagger-style confidentiality. They introduced me to concepts like Markov chains, conditional random fields, Bayesian inferences, and dynamic programming.

In the end, these tech talks inspired me more than they directly informed my algorithms. Honestly, much of the math they described was beyond me. I'm not an engineer by training—in fact, I never took a single math course in college. If there ever was an argument that I should have kept studying the subject beyond high school because there was no telling when I might need it, this was it. I was in over my head.

Yet I wasn't completely lost. When Richard Williamson joined Apple and helped us determine the technical direction for our web browser project, he showed that it was possible to make technical headway by skipping past the problems he couldn't solve in favor of those he could. So, that's what I did.

I started by imagining a picture of my single-letter QWERTY keyboard, and I made a guess about the way I might miss a key I was aiming for.

I supposed that if I wanted to tap the **G** key but missed it to the left and tapped the **F** key instead, I probably meant **G** or **F** more often than I meant **H**. In other words, if I missed the exact key I was aiming for, the one I intended to tap was most likely the next closest key, not some other key farther away. I built the direction of these misses into my algorithm.

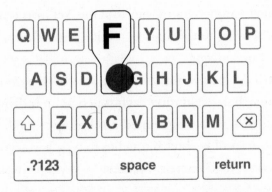

The tap shown popped up the F key, and from its position,
and a guess about what the typist intended, it seems more
likely that if the typist didn't actually mean to type the F key,
then G was probably more likely than any other key.

I also discovered how important it was to give an extra weighting to the keys that actually popped up in the user interface. During the keyboard derby, we learned that the visual of the key appearing under your finger when you tapped was the keyboard's way of telling you what it saw. It was exactly the kind of feedback that can connect people and software. The letter pop-ups on the keyboard created a dialogue between the device and the typist, with the pop-ups playing the role of a backchannel, much like the head nods and "uh-huh" and "mm-hmm" utterances we sprinkle through conversations while we listen to other people speak. The stream of pop-ups let a person know the keyboard was following along, that it was listening.

The information about individual touches was also important to track, so I developed a system for scoring every tap, but it didn't take too long to see that letter-by-letter grading didn't produce better results than just looking at the usage frequency values. How did I know that? I lived on the software. I gave demos to my Purple teammates and they told me. Yet introducing a second level of scoring to the autocorrection algorithm seemed like a step ahead in concept.

Next I tried a more holistic scoring approach based on entire words. Rather than evaluating each touch as an individual event worthy of its own score, I grouped all the taps together. I imagined what a series of keyboard touches to type a word would look like as a picture, a geometrical pattern, a key-tap constellation.

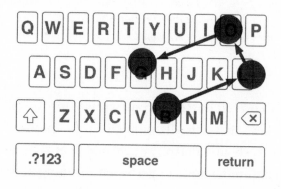

Touches to type the word "blog" form a key-tap constellation, a pattern of touches superimposed on top of the letters on the keyboard.

To make productive use of this concept, I imagined the flawless patterns a superhumanly accurate typist would create with a Wallaby in hand. I pictured asking such an ideal typist to run through the entire dictionary, to type out a full set of error-free, perfectly centered patterns. The resulting collection of constellations would be made of dots positioned in the exact center of every key for every letter for every word in the dictionary.

In my mind, autocorrection became a process of building a pattern from the user's taps and searching the dictionary for the closest-matching pattern from the ideal set. Stated differently, given a keyboarding constellation from a typist—which would inevitably contain noncenter strikes and perhaps some erroneously tapped keys as well—the algorithmic task became finding the keyboarding constellation that looked most similar to the one a superhuman typist would type. The dictionary word corresponding to that ideal constellation would be the word the user meant to type . . . in theory.

To test this, I had to figure out a way to compare these keyboarding patterns to each other. As before, when I did a cursory examination of mathematics texts, I couldn't make sense of data fitting or graph matching techniques that looked something like what I needed. I was unable to understand the formulas and explanations. I was in over my head, and again, I had to think of something simple.

I imagined how much I would need to "nudge" each of the dots in a picture of a typing pattern to make it look exactly like one of the ideal patterns from the dictionary. For each pattern comparison, I added up all the nudges. The closest match was the one that required the fewest nudges. Luckily for me, calculating these nudges was elementary school stuff. It was like getting a map of a grid layout for a city and counting the number of streets and avenues I would need to walk to get between two addresses, a measure sometimes called a Manhattan distance.

This is what my nudges were, a counting up of the geometrical skew required to move a tap a typist made until it matched a dot in a dictionary pattern. A big sum of nudges was a big amount of skew, and indicated a poor match. A small number of nudges indicated a small skew, and was a good match. I gave a name to this operation of comparing patterns and summing nudges: the *pattern skew algorithm.*

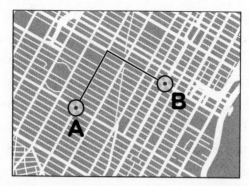

It takes eleven "nudges" on streets and four on avenues to get from point A to point B on this map of Manhattan. Fifteen nudges in all.

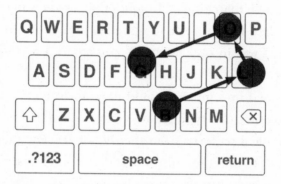

The pattern for a person trying to type the word "blog."

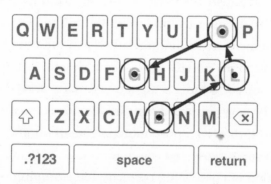

The ideal pattern in the dictionary for "blog," with perfect center-strike touches on all the keys.

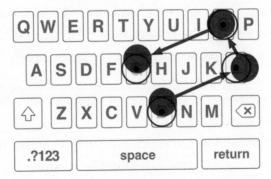

When the two are overlaid, it shows how a little nudging is necessary to make the pattern for the typing look like the ideal one from the dictionary, but not too much. This is a pretty good match.

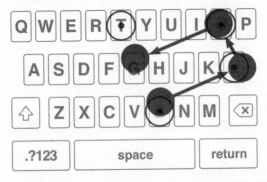

You can see the ideal pattern for the word "blot" is the same as the one for the first three letters, but would require a whole lot more nudging for the last letter. The match for "blot" isn't as good as the one for "blog," hence I assumed the typist meant the latter word rather than the former.

As a person typed on the keyboard, the pattern skew algorithm whirred away in my autocorrection code, building patterns, nudging taps, and comparing touches to words in the dictionary. The output of the pattern skew algorithm was a list of dictionary patterns that looked most like what the typist did, and, of course, since each dictionary pattern represented a word, the algorithm also suggested the words the typist most likely meant. By joining up the pattern skew with the usage frequency values, the autocorrection algorithm became this:

- Arrange typed keys in a set of tumblers with their neighboring keys.
- Spin the tumblers to check every letter combination.
- Note the dictionary words found by spinning the tumblers.
- Calculate the pattern skew for every found word.
- Multiply the usage frequency value for each found word with the reciprocal of its pattern skew.
- From all the found words, suggest the one with the greatest multiplied total of usage frequency and pattern skew.[1]

This was the final autocorrection algorithm. Making this "final" declaration sounds like progress, but as should be clear by now, at Apple in general, and on the Purple project in particular, there was always more to do. The initial feedback from my teammate users was positive—the pattern skew algorithm made it much easier to type accurately. Even so, I spent many additional months tuning and optimizing the nudge calculations to improve the typing experience.

As the pattern skew algorithm got better, other text-related tasks soon bubbled to the top of my to-do list. There was the matter of where all this keyboarding would go, the single-line text fields on cards in the Contacts app and the multiline text areas used in places like the Notes app. I wrote code for these user interface widgets, using my WebKit word processing work as the foundation. Dictionary updates were never completely off my radar, and I kept up with those, adding new Apple product names, such as Xserve, and smarts for automatically inserting an apostrophe into "cant" to turn the word into "can't."

I continued to improve the keyboard, and as the months passed, there were fewer and fewer absurd typing errors. Everyone started to get more optimistic about always-on autocorrection. As a feature, the keyboard started to converge. I started getting close to a typing experience Apple could ship in a product.

While I was focused on the keyboard, everyone else on the Purple team had gone through their own periods of development and discovery. Many of these struggles remained invisible to me, because I was so focused on my own difficult work and because of the compartmentalized security mandated by Steve. I know almost nothing about how we developed our phone hardware, the details of the industrial design process, or the negotiations with phone carriers.

When it came to software, I know more, and I was always trying out the work my colleagues were doing, filling the feedback role for them that they played for me with the keyboard.

For example, with MobileSafari, the Purple web browser, pages often appeared tiny when we displayed them to fit the entire screen of our smartphone. It would have been nearly impossible to tap links if your touches had to hit them exactly. So Richard Williamson and another colleague came up a scheme where tapping would spiral out from the exact point of your touch to find links. The closest was deemed the one you meant to activate.

We needed scores of these finely tuned allowances and affordances throughout our software to make our touchscreen operating system intuitive and easy to use.

Did we feel pressure to fill gaps like these in our system? Yes. I handled it by keeping reasonable and regular work hours. If I wasn't battling exhaustion, I could bear up under the stress. At least most of the time. One day, I lost my temper at a colleague over a disagreement about how we should approach a keyboard-related technology problem at a time when the code was still in flux, and I shouted at him to "GET THE F*** OUT OF MY OFFICE!"

One other incident involves Kim Vorrath, who had the pressure-packed job of juggling our software delivery schedule and the ongoing risk assessments associated with our progress. One evening, in a fit of frustration, she slammed the door to her office so hard that the handle mechanism broke, marooning her inside. Why was she so upset? A sufficiently accurate answer is this: The daily grind of working on Purple. Some insignificant issue caused her to boil over. Scott Forstall busted her out by beating the doorknob off with an aluminum baseball bat.

Such drama was uncommon, for me, for Kim, and for the rest of us. Usually we kept the rate of our progress above the level of our stress, mostly because we hit few roadblocks that wouldn't give way to a good idea.

Time passed, and by the autumn of 2006, our Purple software started to converge. We were getting closer to a software system Apple could ship in a product.

We headed toward the holiday season. I was busy in my office one day when everyone on the Purple hallway got called for an impromptu group meeting. This time Kim was the one asking us to gather, and it wasn't because she wanted us to stop what we were doing so she could kick off another all-hands-on-deck, problem-solving tech derby.

No, this time, she had something to demo herself. I walked down a few doors past Henri's office to an open area with comfy chairs and couches outside Kim's office. A few others had heard the call when I did, and we all gathered around her.

She was holding a Purple phone. Untethered. No cable attached to a Mac. The real industrial design. An actual glass screen, not the plastic display of a Wallaby. I had never seen one of these before, and this wasn't a mere model either. It was a working phone. The hardware was powered up and running with all our software loaded onto it. As Kim handed around this late-stage prototype, she pointed out that there were one or two hardware components that weren't final yet, and since they were slightly bulkier than the parts we would manufacture at volume, the top and bottom of the case didn't meet on the lower left corner of the demo device. There was a little gap, maybe two or three millimeters. The Purple phone was converging, but it wasn't completely converged yet.

When Kim passed the prototype to me, she asked me to handle it gingerly. I took it from her. The glass display was striking—far brighter and sharper than the Wallaby screen we'd been staring at for more than a year. I turned the device over in my hand. It felt solid, like it was filled to the brim with the latest technology, and it was. In fact, at that moment, it was overflowing a bit.

I paced back and forth a few times to feel the freedom of movement that came with untethering from a Mac. The Wallaby experience had been about feeling tied down to a computer on a desk with cabling spidering out everywhere. Now, for the first time, as I put the phone in my pocket, I got an idea of what it would be like to use a Purple phone.

Naturally, I was most interested in the keyboard. I typed out a few words in the Notes app. The keyboard worked without a hitch. My autocorrection code stepped in to fix all the mistakes I made. I could have spent all day with the device, trying out everything I could think of, but other people were waiting for their turn. As I handed the device over, I had no question in my mind.

I wanted one.

With this memorable demo, it was obvious we were converging on a smartphone Apple could ship as a product. We were close, but, as with the hardware enclosure that wouldn't quite snap shut, we weren't there yet. In a few more weeks, we would have to be.

The announcement date was already on the calendar, and we'd been heading toward it for much of the previous year. The release plans converged along with the progress of the software and hardware. Apple would tell everyone about Purple at the Macworld conference in early January 2007, and the company would ship the first phones the following June.

This meant I would still have time to fix a few more bugs and add a few more words to the dictionary before people got their hands on the keyboard. Security remained tight up until the last moment, and when I walked into the Moscone Center on keynote day, I still didn't know what Purple would be called. On the tenth of January 2007, the day after the big product introduction, I edited the autocorrection dictionary to add a new word: **iPhone**.

* * *

Every part of working at Apple could be stressful, and though we only rarely beat down doors with baseball bats or ended conversations with shouted four-letter words, once we entered a convergence period, we started dealing with a persistent product development pressure generated by two opposing forces. One was the constant ticking away of time as we moved closer to an unmovable ship date; the other was the variable and ever-changing number of bug reports representing software problems that needed to be fixed.

We used a program called Radar to monitor our bugs, and this flexible, internally developed bug tracker was like our convergence Swiss Army knife. Radar's main purpose was for reporting software defects and tracking their fixes, but a Radar entry could also play other roles in our development organization: an engineer's to-do item, a designer's enhancement request, a project manager's top-level feature with many subfeatures attached to it, or an executive's high-priority issue.

Radar moved to the center of attention once we entered convergence, several months out from the scheduled ship date. Our managers would start watching the number of Radars more closely, and the count was supposed to begin a steady descent toward zero. During convergence, Henri sent out a graph every morning to everyone on the Purple software team, where he plotted Radar bugs against dates, with the release date at the right end of the x-axis. Over time, the meanderings of the daily bug counts drew a squiggly line: More bugs made the line go up, fewer made it go down. We got good at reading this convergence line and taking the temperature of the project through it. We learned to understand convergence behaviors, like the upward spikes in the line after big demos, which weren't as worrisome as they seemed—many demo bugs would be quick and easy to fix— and the stubborn flat lines over many days, which could indicate real trouble, since the number of incoming bugs was matching our fix rate, and that meant convergence might be stalled.

Don Melton often told a story about convergence at Netscape. When his old company was getting ready to ship versions of the Navigator web browser, the goal wasn't zero bugs. Netscape's engineering leaders knew that no sophisticated piece of software was ever truly devoid of defects. Instead, they shot for *zarro boogs*, an intentional mispronunciation of "zero bugs." It was a humorous recognition that they were calling their project "finished" on the ship date, not that they had actually achieved the unattainable ideal of fault-free code, regardless of what a bug database query or a convergence graph might have shown them.[2]

This relationship between bug fixes and release dates raises a question. If convergence was the primary focus of the Purple team in the last few months before the iPhone was announced, does convergence methodology explain why the iPhone turned out so well?

No. Convergence isn't magic. It's a workaday high-tech development practice. Netscape's engineers did bug convergence. It's also what Don and I were doing during our last few days at Eazel, right up until the morning they fired the majority of the staff. Everybody in professional software development does convergence. So, converging a bug list toward zero can't be the elusive ingredient necessary for making excellent products.

The appeal of the iPhone wasn't the result of piling up a bunch of features early on in our project development schedule, opening the requisite number of bugs to track the implementation of those features, and then converging, fixing them one by one as the schedule led us to ship date. Bug squashing might help to make a decent product, but it's not the secret for making a great one.

I'll soon share more of my ideas about what made our Apple approach special, but first, I'll discuss a counternotion, an example of a process that can't produce iPhone-like excellence. For this I turn to Douglas Bowman, a designer with a résumé that includes stints at Twitter and Wired. He also started at Google in 2006, becoming one of its early visual design leaders.* Here's how he justified his departure from the web search firm almost three years later:

> Without a person at (or near) the helm who thoroughly understands the principles and elements of Design, a company eventually runs out of reasons for design decisions ... Without

---

* Bowman started at Google around the same time we were in the Purple hallway at Apple, deep in development on the iPhone.

conviction, doubt creeps in. Instincts fail . . . When a company is filled with engineers, it turns to engineering to solve problems. Reduce each decision to a simple logic problem. Remove all subjectivity and just look at the data. Data in your favor? Ok, launch it. Data shows negative effects? Back to the drawing board. And that data eventually becomes a crutch for every decision . . .

Yes, it's true that a team at Google couldn't decide between two blues, so they're testing 41 shades between each blue to see which one performs better.[3]

Forty-one shades of blue sounds like a lot, but if they were willing to go that far at Google, why not test for a hundred or a thousand? If some data is good, more must be better, right? As Bowman suggests, it isn't.

In this kind of test, commonly referred to in the high-tech industry as an A/B test, the choices are already laid out. In this Google pick-a-blue experiment, the result was always going to be one of those forty-one options. While the A/B test might be a good way to find the single most clickable shade of blue, the dynamic range between best and worst isn't that much. More important, the opportunity cost of running all the trials meant there was less time available for everyone on the development team to dream up a design that people might like two, or three, or ten times more. A/B tests might be useful in finding a color that will get people to click a link more often, but it can't produce a product that feels like a pleasing and integrated whole. There aren't any refined-like responses, and there's no recognition of the need to balance out the choices. Google factored out taste from its design process.

At Apple, we never would have dreamed of doing that, and we never staged any A/B tests for any of the software on the iPhone. When it came to choosing a color, we picked one. We used our good taste—and our knowledge of how to make software accessible to people with visual difficulties related to color perception—and we moved on.

Or did we? Well, yes and no. We always made quick choices about small details, but we were always willing to reconsider previous decisions. We took more time with bigger questions, but never too much. We were always mindful of making steady progress. I certainly absorbed this lesson from the earliest days of Safari development, when Don and I were in our six-week funk and Richard produced his two-day demo to shake us out of it. Maintaining headway toward a goal was a key part of the way Apple did software development. It's fair to say we were always in a convergence period of a sort, even though we didn't think of it in that way. Yet our forward movement always had a destination. We were constantly converging toward the next demo.

The concrete and specific demos I described in chapter 6 were catalysts for creative decisions. They forced us to make judgments about what was good, what needed changes or improvements, and what should be deleted. We habitually converged on demos, then we allowed demo feedback to cause a fresh divergence, one that we immediately sought to close for the follow-on demo.

The next demo was never far away, and often it was quite close. In the case of the Giggly Demo for Richard, it took me mere minutes to edit the code to turn on full-time autocorrection. We were continuously producing fresh rounds of software like this, to test our latest ideas and assumptions. As a whole, a succession of demos, feedback, and follow-up demos created a progression of variation and selection that shaped our products over time.

It's a Darwinian process, and not surprisingly, Charles Darwin himself was unequivocal about the potential and power of adding up incremental modifications down a line of generations. In the first chapter of *On the Origin of Species*, before he introduced his then-radical concept of natural selection, Darwin began with a lengthy discussion of artificial selection, building on the familiarity his nineteenth-century audience had with animal husbandry:

> But when we compare the dray-horse and race-horse, the dromedary and camel, the various breeds of sheep fitted either for cultivated land or mountain pasture, with the wool of one breed good for one purpose, and that of another breed for another purpose; when we compare the many breeds of dogs, each good for man in very different ways . . . we must, I think, look further than to mere variability. We cannot suppose that all the breeds were suddenly produced as perfect and as useful as we now see them; indeed, in several cases, we know that this has not been their history. The key is man's power of accumulative selection: nature gives successive variations; man adds them up in certain directions useful to him . . . It is the magician's wand, by means of which he may summon into life whatever form and mould he pleases.[4]

As best we could on the Purple hallway, we sought to wield a similar magician's wand to mold our products, building variation into our demos, keeping the strong aspects and discarding the weak, and making the next demo based on those decisions. With our Darwinian demo methodology, we had a huge advantage over artificially selecting breeders and the glacially slow accumulations of genetic improvements that drive natural selection. Working in software meant we could move fast. We could make changes whenever we wanted, and we did. We created new demos that were concretely and specifically targeted to be better than the previous one. We constructed Hollywood backlots around these demos to provide context and to help us suspend our disbelief about the often nonexistent system surrounding the feature or app that was the focus of our attention. We gave each other feedback, both as initial impressions and after living on the software to test the viability of the ideas and quality of the associated implementations. We gathered up action items for the next iteration, and then we forged ahead toward the next demo. I've given a name to this continuing progression of demo → feedback → next demo: *creative selection*.

As I've said elsewhere, we didn't have a formal name for what we were doing while we were doing it. We were always so focused on the next demo, the next review session, the next time we were scheduled to show progress to Steve. Our iterative working method was like the air—something all around us all the time, something we were always aware of on some level, something it didn't make sense to question. Yet we took our approach for granted more than we should have.

There are innumerable ways creative selection can become bogged down, since this working method must be applied consistently over a period of time to yield results. Consequently, our success was as much about what we didn't do as what we did. Mostly we avoided falling into any of the typical product development traps common in Silicon Valley and that, I expect, occur often in other kinds of creative organizations and businesses.

For example, we didn't take two-hour coffee breaks or hold daylong offsite confabs to talk about projects without examples to ground the discussion—we didn't have lengthy discussions about whose imaginary puppy was cuter.

We didn't shuffle around printed specifications or unchanging paper mock-ups for weeks on end, waiting for an epiphany that would jump us directly from an early-stage concept to a complete product design, hoping we could somehow flip the ratio of inspiration to perspiration Thomas Edison spoke about, the relationship between the time it takes to get an idea and the amount of hard work it takes to transform that idea into something real. I learned my lesson on this count, and in my Apple career, never again did I spend a week of my time to make anything like that fifty-step *Building the Lizard* document I described in chapter 2.

We didn't have an imbalance between influence and involvement, where a senior leader might try to mimic the commanding role of Steve Jobs without the corresponding level of personal engagement. Detached high-level managers making all the key decisions is such a widespread affliction that it has its own internet meme, the Seagull Manager. It describes a top executive who is rarely around but flies in occasionally and unexpectedly from who knows where, lands on your beach, squawks noisily, flaps its wings all over the place, launches itself back into the air, circles overhead, drops a big poop on everyone, and then flies away, leaving the rest of the team to clean up the mess, figure out what it all meant, and wonder what to do about the inevitable follow-up visit.[5]

We didn't establish large, cutting-edge software research departments sequestered from, and with a tenuous connection to, the designers and engineers responsible for creating and shipping the real products. Steve Jobs famously disbanded such an organization at Apple, the Advanced Technology Group, shortly after he reasserted control over the company in 1997.

These kinds of anti-patterns can prevent creative selection from functioning correctly, since they block the steady accumulation of positive change while developing a product. They're not the only ways the process can break down. You could build and release products without ever living on them to see if they're any good, as we did with Nautilus and our online services at Eazel. You could hold demo meetings and then adjourn them without deciding what to do next, a mistake that interrupts the chain of criticism that provides the logical connection from demo to demo. You could assign oversized project teams to the tasks one or two people could handle, a fault that can lead to muddled communications and a dilution of each person's ability to make a difference. You could have conflicting lines of authority and fail to ever reach universally recognized final decisions. You could design for looks, or for fashion, or for some abstract ideal instead of designing for how a product works. You could stage A/B tests to help make simple decisions, as was done, apparently, to choose colors at Google.

We managed to steer clear of all such pitfalls. If I were to take a stab at explaining the *why*, I would say that our clarity of purpose kept us on track, in much the same way that Vince Lombardi won football games and Steve Jobs pushed us to make a speedy first version of Safari. Since our focus on making great products never wavered—if for no other reason than that's what Steve demanded—perhaps concentrating keenly on what to do helped us to block out what *not* to do.

Whatever the explanation for how we got started, as we had success with creative selection, it became self-reinforcing. We evolved and improved our process as we produced good results with it. We took a page right out of Darwin, recasting his concepts to suit our product development goals.

We always started small, with some inspiration. We made demos. We mixed in feedback. We listened to guidance from smart colleagues. We blended in variations. We honed our vision.

We followed the initial demo with another and then another. We improved our demos in incremental steps. We evolved our work by slowly converging on better versions of the vision. Round after round of creative selection moved us step by step from the spark of an idea to a finished product.

If I extend the Darwinian metaphor, then creative selection was supplemented by the selection pressures we created to help shape our progress from demo to demo, in the phase of deciding what to vary. From its beginnings, Apple always had a characteristic sense of what to select for, a viewpoint on which ideas were strong, and this helped to define the conditions under which the creative selection process unfolded. In the next chapter, I'll describe this aspect of Apple-style product development in more detail.

9

The Intersection

When Steve introduced the iPhone about forty-one minutes[*]
into his keynote at Macworld 2007, he clicked to a slide showing
a dark Apple logo eclipsing the sun, then he said, "This is a day
I've been looking forward to for two and a half years. Every once
in a while, a revolutionary product comes along that changes
everything."[1]

---

[*] If you ever wondered why iPhones and iPads often show 9:41 as the time on
the lock screen and in the status bar in ads and posters, the reason is that
the Apple keynotes were often planned out to do the biggest product introduction about forty minutes into the show. (Note that online videos of these
presentations omit clips of copyrighted material from music, TV shows, and
movies, so the times are off.) The idea was to have the time in the marketing photos of the new product match, or at least be close to, the actual time
in the hall at the moment of the reveal. So it was for the iPhone. After that,
using 9:41 became a tradition, perhaps a superstition. Apple Watch uses
10:09 for a totally different reason—that's just how the designers thought
the hands looked best, especially on analog faces. Go figure.

I was in the audience on that day, and while I was excited about the big on-stage reveal that everyone on the Purple project had been working toward with such determination, I wasn't sure what to think about Steve's claim. He had a conviction about the iPhone in that moment; I only had hopes for it.

For the previous year and a half, I had been treating Purple as a prototype rather than a product, and I was usually paying attention to the parts that didn't work quite right yet—developing features, fixing bugs, pushing for the next improvement, aiming toward the next demo. It's difficult to maintain a wider perspective in the midst of making; you have to make sure each individual demo feedback and response cycle eventually adds up to something more.

"The Intersection," the title of this chapter, was an idea that helped us. It speaks to the way Apple valued expertise in both *technology* and *liberal arts*. We used this notion to guide our efforts as we developed and lived on our gadgets, so that they turned out to be more than an agglomeration of the latest CPUs, sensors, and software manufactured at scale. We hoped to make our products meaningful and useful to people.

Unlike the unspoken idea of creative selection, we *did* talk about "working at the intersection" among ourselves. There was even a formal Apple University* course on the topic—a moderated half-day session to discuss melding technology and liberal arts, the reasons it might be difficult to work at this intersection, and why it was essential to keep trying, since the effort lay at the core of the Apple notion of a great product.

Not only was the intersection freely discussed inside the company, but oddly for Apple, the discussion didn't stop at the

---

*Apple University is an internal company-sponsored training department whose mission is to capture, communicate, understand, and preserve Apple best practices.

edge of the Cupertino campus. Steve Jobs told everyone what he thought about this topic himself, on stage, during the keynote presentation to announce the original iPad:

> The reason that Apple is able to create products like the iPad is because we've always tried to be at the intersection of technology and liberal arts, to be able to get the best of both, to make extremely advanced products from a technology point of view, but also have them be intuitive, easy to use, fun to use, so that they really fit the users. The users don't have to come to them, they come to the user.[2]

The notion of working at the intersection goes back far into Apple history. Steve used it to explain why the original Macintosh in 1984 had proportionally spaced fonts instead of the monospace teletype-like characters typical on computers of the day.[3] From that time forward, working at the intersection became a summation of the qualities Apple aspired to instill in its products. It went beyond fonts, colors, and the visual design elements you might think of when you hear the word "art" in liberal arts.

The effort extended to all the senses. I wanted the iPhone keyboard click to evoke the clack of a typewriter key striking a page and ultimately achieved this by striking my pencil on the edge of my desk. I'd been inspired by a story I heard of how Ben Burtt, the sound designer for the first *Star Wars* movie, made the sound effect for blaster shots by recording hammer strikes on a guy wire for an antenna tower.*[4]

---

* I produced two options for the keyboard click sound. I started with the same captured pencil-desk-strike sample and made two variations by processing them in Macromedia SoundEdit 16. I called one *tick* and the other *tock*. They were demoed to Steve, he chose *tock*, and that was that. As far as I know, that sound lasted unchanged through several versions of iOS and was the pinnacle of my career as a recording artist.

Working at the intersection is not only about honing details so that an individual icon, animation, or sound achieves an aesthetic ideal in isolation. Liberal arts elements and state-of-the-art technology must combine, and the end result can be judged only holistically, by evaluating how the product fits the person.

The three brief stories that follow illustrate how we did this throughout the development of the iPhone. They describe the way some of the features and attributes of the iPhone software came to be and demonstrate specific instances of our attempts to work at the intersection.

The First-Ever iPhone Game Was Serious Fun

When I started on the iPhone team in the summer of 2005, I was a complete novice with touch software. When I was issued my first handheld Wallaby, it was a novel experience to write a program, launch it on my Mac, and see the graphics for the app show up on the prototype touchscreen. I'd take my hands off the keyboard of my Mac, pick up the Wallaby, and then tap icons, choose rows in scrolling lists, and navigate around in apps. Everyone else on the Purple hallway was doing the same thing, testing out what it was like to interact with software and imagery on the Wallaby using our fingers.

All of us on the software team were trying to solve our own technical problems, trying to bootstrap apps like Mail, Safari, Notes, and SpringBoard, and before long, we started asking each other the same "big" question: How large should we make objects on the screen so they're easy to tap? Tap targets needed to be small enough so that a single screen displayed enough content to be useful but large enough that you could confidently tap what you wanted. Beyond that, we didn't have more detailed notions about the sizes of onscreen objects.

It was especially important to get this right for SpringBoard, the program that displayed the home screen icons. These rounded-off squares represented all the apps on the device. Tapping a SpringBoard icon launched an app that took over the entire screen. Tapping the correct icon was satisfying, since it made the whole iPhone interface become a note taker, a web browser, or a calendar. Moving from task to task happened at the speed of thought. Tapping the wrong app icon could be jarring, like realizing you picked up a fork instead of a spoon only after dipping it in a bowl of soup.

For SpringBoard, this ergonomic issue reduced to finding the optimal easy-to-tap size for such an icon on the home screen. We didn't know what this might be, and the first few Purple demo sessions with Wallabies gave us some insight into the range in anatomy and dexterity we could expect to find in the general population.

Scott Forstall had long, spidery fingers that narrowed to small fingertips. He could arch his thumbs high above the Wallaby display and then move them up and down with nearly mechanical precision, like rocker arms in the valve train of an engine. Scott was genetically predisposed to be amazingly accurate with his touchscreen taps, and he could confidently target and hit the smallest onscreen user interface elements without thinking about it.

In contrast, Greg Christie's hands shook. His fingers were especially juddery if he had just taken a walk outside to smoke a cigarette. If one of us on the software development team gave Greg a too-small icon that was too difficult for him to tap, he would try anyway, and when he failed, he would heave his characteristic sigh—his loud, long, disgruntled New Yorker's sigh—to express his $#!&% frustration that he couldn't use the thing you handed him. Greg would be in the right too. Remember,

Steve Jobs didn't say products should thwart the user; he said products should "come to the user."

We expected the variance in the entire population would be larger than we'd seen with just Scott and Greg, but their differing user experiences provided us with proof early on in our development process that one of the most important user interactions for the iPhone rested on this question: What's the best size for a home screen icon?

Scott Herz, one of my Purple teammates, soon gave us the answer. He wrote an app and circulated it around the Purple team. There wasn't much to it. The app launched showing a very large Start button. After tapping that button, the screen would go blank for a moment, then a box would appear somewhere on the display. The goal was to tap the box. After you tapped, whether you succeeded or failed, and after another momentary blank, another box would appear somewhere else. Only this next box would be a different size, maybe larger, maybe smaller. Tap the box. Tap the box. Tap the box.

Honestly, it was fun. Like a game. After twenty or so boxes and taps, the "game" would end, and the app would show you your score: how many boxes you hit and how many you missed. Behind the scenes, the software tracked the sizes of the boxes and their location. Since it was a fun game to play . . . *ahem* . . . a serious test program to gather essential touchscreen usability data, the Herz tap app made a quick round of the Purple hallway. Within a few days, we had quite a bit of information about tap-target sizes and accuracy.

The results of Scott's game showed that if we placed a box on the screen that was fifty-seven pixels square, then we could put it at any location—high, low, left, or right. If we did that, then everybody could tap the box comfortably, with near 100 percent accuracy.

Scott's game gave us the answer we were looking for. The tap targets for home screen icons on the original iPhone were fifty-seven pixels square.

Smooth

One of the key concepts of the iPhone user interface is *direct manipulation*. This idea refers to giving software objects some of the same attributes and behaviors as physical objects, enabling people to interact with digital bits as if they were real-world items.

Here's an example. Picture yourself sitting in an office. You have two objects on your desk, a piece of paper and a manila file folder. If you want to put the paper into the folder, you reach out with your hand, pick up the paper, and move it into the folder, perhaps tipping the folder open a little as you do so to make the filing go more smoothly. Acting directly on an object produces a result, and there's a constant flow of sensory feedback—visual, tactile, auditory—to help you monitor your progress.

Throughout the history of computing, such humdrum activities have never been that easy. For decades, computers compelled users to type text commands to interact with digital objects, and this conceptual distance made it more difficult to get things done. On a UNIX computer, a command to move a document to a folder might be:

```
mv paper.txt folder
```

To issue this command, you would have to know the name of the "move" program—cryptically shortened to "mv"—and remember that the thing you want to move comes first, the destination second. Command line interfaces like this make computing abstract, distant, and nonintuitive for everyone but the geeks who think it's cool to learn all the arcane incantations. For everyone else, the (correct) reaction is: "Yech!"

Back in the 1980s, Apple had helped to change this with the Macintosh. The graphical user interface of the Mac, with its mouse and icons, offered a more direct experience. Interacting with an object meant moving the mouse to the object you wanted. Picking it up was done with a click and hold on the mouse button, a gesture that evoked grasping the object with your hand. Dropping the object into a folder meant moving the object on top of an icon of a folder and releasing the mouse button. All these conventions made computing friendlier, and they helped to introduce the concept of direct manipulation: You could see icons on the screen that represented the objects available to interact with, and you could point at them with the mouse.

Apple didn't invent direct manipulation—a computer scientist named Ben Shneiderman did in 1982[5]—but the Mac was quick to popularize it. Early on, Apple was aware of this cutting-edge human–computer interaction research, understood the core technological concept, built a system around it, and, starting in January 1984, bundled it into a product that people could buy. The Mac and the mouse helped to establish the Apple tradition of using new technology to solve age-old interaction problems, and this approach served as inspiration for many years to come.

Even before the Purple project started, a few designers and engineers at Apple believed finger-based multitouch software had the same potential as the mouse. They believed that touch could move the interaction model of computing to the next level of directness. Their hope was that multitouch could eliminate the need for a mouse altogether. See an object on the screen? Just reach out and touch it with your finger.

Imran Chaudhri was one of these early multitouch proponents, and he helped to supply the design inspiration that transformed this new technology into a product.

The software design group at Apple called itself Human Interface for a reason. Humans were the focus, and, as much as anyone I've ever met, Imran believed products must serve people. Like so many other influential people at Apple, Imran's work was a sharply focused reflection of his personality. He had a smoothness, a low-key kind of cool that is vexingly difficult to describe but is communicated instantly in person. After talking to my wife for years about Imran, she finally got a chance to meet him at an Apple-sponsored party to celebrate one of our yearly software releases. Afterward, she said to me, "Yeah, I see what you mean about Imran. He's got charisma."

Charisma. Yeah, Imran had that. Yet, unlike Steve Jobs, the most famously charismatic person in Apple history, Imran never got in anybody's face or dressed people down. Rather, he always spoke very softly. His manner drew you in close. While his hushed voice demanded attention, it had nothing to do with shyness. Indeed, Imran always knew exactly what he wanted, and he was perfectly clear when it came to communicating his design goals for the products we were developing.

From the start of our work on Purple, Imran had a vision for how multitouch user interfaces should behave. To illustrate what he meant, say to an assembled group of Purple software engineers and designers, Imran would clear a space on a flat surface in front of him, a table or a desk, then he would place a single sheet of paper down and extend his index finger to touch the middle of the sheet. Then he would begin sliding his finger and the paper around as an inseparable unit, swirling the sheet around and around, the lockstep movement of his gesture and the object he was manipulating modeling the fluidity and responsiveness he wanted for the iPhone user interface.

"Here, ladies and gents," he would say with his kindly English accent, motioning with a nod of his head toward his demonstration, "it should work like this."

Imran used this piece of paper gliding around under his finger to show how iPhone direct manipulation should feel, and for him, the feeling of it was essential.* He believed the pixels on the iPhone screen needed to remain pinned under your finger as if they were real objects. He wanted people to be convinced that the movement of the digital bits on the screen was the result of physical forces—just like his index finger and the paper. Since the real sheet of paper never paused or stuttered, his argument went, why should the pixels?

This feeling had a purpose. Imran wanted you to feel free to concentrate on the articles you read on the web as you panned to the bottom of the page, to bond with your friends as you sat together and swiped through photos of a recent vacation, and to reflect on your emotions or state of mind as you scrolled through music to choose the perfect song for the moment. He believed that if the imagery on the screen never slipped out from under your touch, you would forget about the technology and focus on the experiences the device opened up to you.

---

*It's customary practice in the high-tech world to use paper drawings and cut-outs as prototyping tools when designing and developing software. One of the prime arguments in favor of paper prototypes is that they're quick to make. On the Purple project, we didn't use them. The simplest explanation I can offer is that the low fidelity of paper prototypes made it too difficult for us to evaluate how an app or interaction would work in a multitouch system. I honestly think this direct manipulation demonstration by Imran is the only meaningful paper demo ever done for the original iPhone.

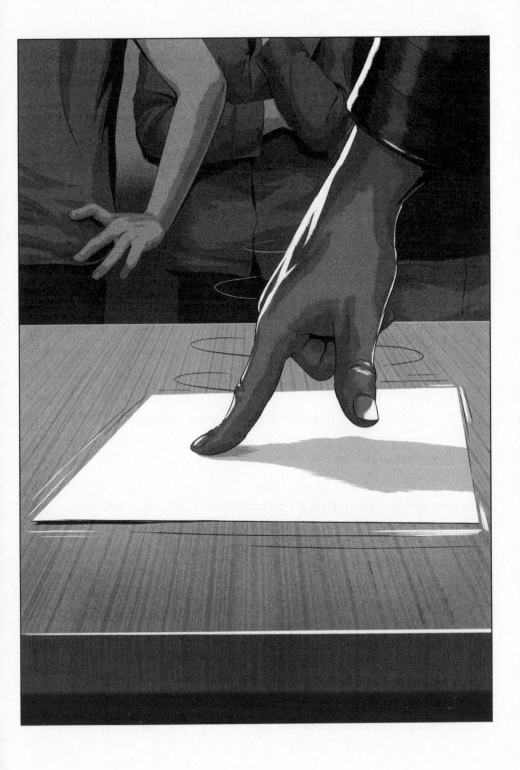

Lightening the Load

Time for a quiz. Read the following instructions carefully. Choose one of the listing challenges shown. Don't write anything down. Use only your mind to keep track of the items as you think of them. Pick your favorite and go.

1. The names of the dwarves from *Snow White and the Seven Dwarves*
2. The first seven prime numbers greater than ten
3. Seven countries in Europe with names that start with a vowel

How did you do? Maybe you're a big Disney fan, so that one was easy, or perhaps you're a math whiz or a geography expert. Even if you are, and even if you didn't write anything down, I bet you used your fingers to keep count. If you gave in to this temptation, then you cheated a little, but I don't blame you. We all need a crutch like that when trying to juggle this many items in our minds at once.

This quiz illustrates a concept I've mentioned a few times in this book: mental load. It's a fact that our working memory has hard limits, and there has been decades of study to understand the bounds of our cognitive capabilities, extending back to the psychology paper titled *The Magical Number Seven, Plus or Minus Two: Some Limits on Our Capacity for Processing Information*, published by George A. Miller of Harvard University in 1956.[6] Miller wanted to quantify the constraints on our short-term mental capacities. He found we can hold only around seven items in our working memories at once. That's it. Trying to handle more than sevenish things in our minds simultaneously requires us to start making chunks or, as Miller puts it, to create "groups of items that go together." For example, I have no trouble remembering these seven colors in order: red, white, blue, cyan, yellow, magenta, black, since the first three are the colors of the American flag and the last four are the colors commonly used in offset lithography. I can chunk them together easily because of my nationality and my knowledge of printing processes. Even for random data, it's easier to recall these nine numbers, 984–313–552, than these, 847620475, just because of the visual prechunking cues provided by the dashes. However, if we can't free up slots in our mind by making chunks when a lot of information is coming at us, we become overloaded, and once our working memory is filled, we begin to make more errors and less accurate judgments. Our ability to function falls off fast.

My experience making products has taught me that this limit is real. Interacting with technology, especially when it's new or tricky, creates the same kind of burden as my listing quiz. We soon hit our mental boundaries, and it doesn't take much to knock our minds off course when we're navigating in a sea of complexity. We can easily get lost in software features, and if that happens, we don't have enough intellectual capacity to find solid ground and focus on what we're actually trying to do.

To make products more approachable, designers must lighten the load on people trying to use the things they make. Even small simplifications make a difference. The good news is that I think it's almost always possible to streamline tasks to make them less taxing.

For example, here is the listing quiz again, tuned to make it easier to accomplish. Get a sheet of paper, something to write with, then pick your favorite one of these three modified challenges, and go:

1. The names of any seven Disney characters

2. The first seven prime numbers
3. Any seven countries in Europe

Of course, the lists are now easier to make, but don't be fooled by the contrived circumstance of a quiz in a book. Similar possibilities to simplify almost always exist in real product development, and at Apple, we went looking for them. My story in chapter 1 is an example. When I demoed two potential iPad keyboard layouts—the more-keys layout designed by Bas and the bigger-keys option I made—Steve Jobs realized we could eliminate the choice, reduce the number of things iPad users might try to juggle in their minds while typing text, and so make the product easier to use. These opportunities weren't always easy to see. It wasn't always obvious what parts of a system, if jettisoned, would trigger a genuine less-is-more response.

Throughout the latter stages of keyboard development for the original iPhone, I continued to tune and refine the text entry software, and as we got closer to the Macworld keynote date, I thought we were done with big changes to the system. Then, in November, about six weeks before Steve Jobs stepped on stage to announce the iPhone to everyone, Scott Forstall told me to ditch the suggestion bar, the horizontal area immediately above the keyboard that displayed three or four tappable words the autocorrection system thought you might be trying to type.

The suggestion bar was a vestige from the keyboard-derby-winning design, and Scott decided we didn't need it. As the autocorrection system got better, thanks to the pattern skew algorithm and my dictionary enhancements, the top autocorrection suggestion was almost always the one people wanted, and the system displayed it directly under the typed word. Scott considered the number of places a person might look while typing— around the blinking insertion point was one place, and focusing

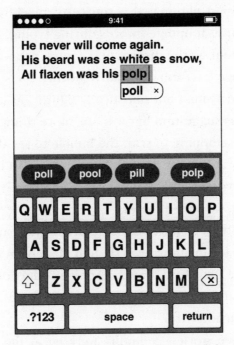

For the release of the original iPhone, we removed the suggestion
bar from above the keyboard. After that, autocorrections only
appeared right under the word with the insertion point in it.

attention on fingers or thumbs to tap the keyboard itself was a second place. Having the suggestion bar created a third place to look—one too many. The suggestion bar increased the mental overhead of the keyboard system, in a way similar to adding a quiz condition that European country names must start with a vowel. Scott thought the suggestion bar was less of an aid and more of a distraction, so he had me get rid of it.*

---

* The suggestion bar returned to the iPhone with the Japanese keyboard due to the specific needs of entering Japanese text, and in iOS 8, the QuickType keyboard brought the suggestion bar back to the iPhone keyboard for many more languages, including English. Although I was still at Apple at the time, I wasn't involved in the development of QuickType.

This decision eliminated a source of pixel-flashing in the suggestion bar as it updated words during typing, it made room for more content on the display, and contrary to what you might think, our user tests showed that removing the suggestion bar actually led to a small but statistically significant *increase* in typing speed. The suggestion bar was one more thing for our mind to juggle, and stopping to scan the bubble to see if it contained the word we wanted was actually slower than just continuing to pound out keys and letting autocorrection clean it all up. So, at Scott's urging, we edited for less.

When Scott asked me to cut a feature like the suggestion bar, it didn't make me grumpy, even though I had been working hard on the feature for over a year. As Apple product developers, we were always happy to improve our user experiences by lightening the load of our software.*

These three stories exemplify working at the intersection, and they show how important it was for us to balance technology with liberal arts. Scott Herz found the threshold that made targets comfortable for people to tap. Imran wanted smoothness in the user interface because it helped to connect the pixels on the screen to people's real-world experiences. Scott Forstall told me to eliminate the keyboard suggestion bar to lighten the mental load on people.

Determining comfort levels, pursuing smoothness, and reducing mental load are examples of the kinds of ergonomic,

---

*Here's an answer key for the first version of the listing quiz. In addition to Grumpy and Happy, whom I mention in this paragraph, Snow White's other five diminutive companions were Bashful, Sneezy, Sleepy, Doc, and of course, Dopey. The first seven prime numbers greater than ten are 11, 13, 17, 19, 23, 29, and 31. At the time of writing, the list of European country names that start with a vowel are: Albania, Andorra, Armenia, Austria, Azerbaijan, Estonia, Iceland, Ireland, Italy, Ukraine, and the United Kingdom.

perceptual, and psychological effects we often aimed for, and in each case, honing and tuning technology to a high level became the means to achieve people-centered results.

There are many more examples of our attempts to mix technology and liberal arts at the intersection, but there isn't space here to tell anecdotes to cover them all, so here are just a few more Purple-era examples in an extra-brief form.

Warp: You might think that when you tap the iPhone screen, the tip of your finger touches the screen, but that isn't so. Given the curved shape of our fingertips, the point of impact is actually lower, and it's this spot on your finger that contacts the touchscreen first. The software modifies the geometry of your actual touch points, shifting or *warping* them upward to account for this difference, giving you a sense that your touch targeting is right on.

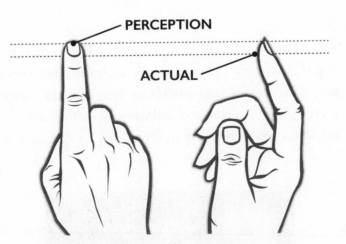

The distance between the perception and actual lines may not seem like a lot, but if the software didn't warp touches, it would feel like the touchscreen isn't accurate.

Charged Buttons: The actual geometry for the back button in the top navigation bar is too small to tap comfortably, so the button is *charged,* which means the active area the software recognizes for tapping is larger than the visual area for the button.

The visual representation of the Back button . . .

. . . was smaller than its active area. An approximation of the enlarged active area, the result of "charging" the button, is shown by the light shading.

Child's Play: The original slide-to-unlock feature helped to prevent you from unintentionally activating features when the phone was in your pocket or bag, and the slider-and-channel user interface to unlock was sufficiently intuitive that when Imran handed an iPhone to his daughter for the

The slide to unlock control was intuitive enough that a child could use it.

first time—she was about three years old—she looked at the screen for a moment and, with no prompting other than what the software showed her, she slid the control and unlocked the phone. No problem.

Can't Miss: Tapping within the keyboard rectangle always resulted in a key activation. Since the keys do not touch each other, either visually or at the software level, it was possible to tap within the bounds of the keyboard but not hit a key. However, I decided that if a typist tapped on the keyboard, the goal was to type, so I always gave a result. In the case of a miss, I activated the geometrically closest key to the tap.

I could go on and on about features and decisions similar to these, including how the physical home button had a comforting secondary role as an always-present escape hatch for people who got lost or confused in an app, and how animations communicated the app model—launching and suspending zoomed in and out, while navigating deeper into an app's content slid side to side.

Indeed, I could go on, and if you're willing to read legalese, you can too. I refer you to United States Patent 7,479,949, sometimes called the '949 Patent when dealing with Apple lawyers, or just the iPhone Patent when not. Its formal title is Touch Screen Device, Method, and Graphical User Interface for Determining Commands by Applying Heuristics.[7] This document is Apple's official statement on the novel software features and functions on the original iPhone, a 358-page patent that is dense with diagrams, embodiments, and claims. This filing aimed to provide an exhaustive rundown of the multitouch user interface, with sections delving into the nitty-gritty of numerous specific interactions. For example, here's a brief excerpt describing how finger movements across the touchscreen might be interpreted in certain situations:

> In some embodiments, the direction of translation corresponds directly to the direction of finger movement; in some embodiments, however, the direction of translation is mapped from the direction of finger movement in accordance with a rule. For example, the rule may state that if the direction of finger movement is within Y degrees of a standard axis, the direction of translation is along the standard axis, and otherwise the direction of translation is substantially the same as the direction of finger movement.[8]

It's curious how lawyerly descriptions of the iPhone fail to communicate any of the good feelings we, on the Purple development team, tried so hard to put in. But, of course, patents are not written to put smiles on people's faces. Yet, even at the highest level, the '949 Patent did get at something fundamental about working at the intersection. Right in the title of the patent, there's mention of one of our building blocks: heuristics.

We used the word "heuristics" to describe aspects of software development that tip toward the liberal arts. Its counterpart, "algorithms," was its alter ego on the technical side. Heuristics and algorithms are like two sides of the same coin. Both are specific procedures for making software do what it does: taking input, applying an operation, and producing output. Yet each had a different purpose.

Algorithms produce quantifiable results, where progress is defined by measurements moving in a predetermined direction, as in the case of the nearly yearlong effort to improve the performance of Safari. The Page Load Test reported how our code was doing, and it delivered this result in one number, the average time to load a page. All along, we had a clear goal for this number—to reduce it. This was never in question. Faster times were better. The same kind of thing can be said of the insertion point movement in a word processor. When the blinking caret is placed at the end of an English word in the middle of a line, tapping the space key once should insert a space and move the insertion point to the right by one character. There's no dispute about whether this is correct or not. If a space key press doesn't insert a space and advance the insertion point in this situation, it's a bug. Algorithms are like this. They're objective.

Heuristics also have a measurement or value associated with them—the duration for an animation or the red-green-blue values for an onscreen color, but there isn't a similar "arrow of improvement" that always points the same way. Unlike evaluating algorithms, heuristics are harder to nail down. For instance, how quickly should a scrolling list glide to a stop after you've flicked it? We always made demos to evaluate the possibilities. I would often sit down with an HI designer like Bas or Imran to make preliminary decisions about gestures and animations, then we would review our preliminary choices in larger groups, then the whole team would live on the results over time. We used the same scheme to develop heuristics for the whole system.

How long should it take for an app icon to animate up from its place on the home screen to fill the entire display? How far should you have to drag your finger on the screen for it to be possible to interpret the touch as a swipe gesture? How much should a two-finger pinch gesture allow you to zoom in on an image in the Photos app? The answers to all of these questions were numbers, and might be 0.35 seconds for the app animation, or 30 pixels for the swipe gesture, or 4x for photo zooming, but the number was never the point. The values themselves weren't provably better in any engineering sense. Rather, the numbers represented sensible defaults, or pleasing effects, or a way to give people what they meant rather than what they did. It takes effort to find what these things are, which is appropriate, since the etymological root of "heuristic" is *eureka*, which (of course) comes from the Greek and means "to find." This is where that word, "eureka," actually figured into our development process, since good heuristics don't come in brilliant flashes, but only after patient searches, and it wasn't always clear to us that we had found the right heuristic even when we had. We arrived at our final decisions only with judgment and time. Heuristics are like this. They're subjective.

We used algorithms and heuristics like they were the left and right sides of our collective product development brain. Employing each involved an interplay of craft and taste, and we always tried to strike the correct balance. Algorithms and heuristics must coordinate to make a great high-tech product. Fast web page loads, correct insertion point movement, efficient code, lovely animations, intuitive gestures, and well-considered built-in behaviors are all essential in a product like the iPhone. Our goal was comfortable technology and computer-enabled liberal arts, a combination of both.

However, it's crucial to make the right call about whether to use an algorithm or a heuristic in a specific situation. This is why the Google experiment with forty-one shades of blue seems so foreign to me, accustomed as I am to the Apple approach. Google used an A/B test to make a color choice. It used a single predetermined value criterion and defined it like so: The best shade of blue is the one that people clicked most often in the test. This is an algorithm.

At Apple, we never considered the notion of an algorithmically correct color. We used demos to pick colors and animation timings, and we put our faith in our sense of taste. When we went looking for the right "finger movement in accordance with a rule," as mentioned in the excerpt I included from the '949 Patent, we made a subjective call. We developed heuristics.

At the same time, we weren't overly touchy-feely about everything. Creating optimized algorithms was a significant part of developing the software for the iPhone, as it was for making Safari before it. What was important was that there remained a tension and flow between the algorithms and heuristics—making the correct choices to lean toward technology or liberal arts could be complicated.

For example, sometimes we used heuristics to temper algorithms. In keyboard autocorrection, the pattern skew algorithm could *always* find the closest-matching dictionary word for any sequence of letters. Imagine someone typing **oooorr**, perhaps to add an elongated stress on the word "or" in the midst of making the choice between two wonderful options (e.g., we could have three-scoop ice cream sundaes oooorr chocolate seven-layer cake for dessert). Whatever the case, the word "oooorr" isn't in the dictionary, nor does it look very much like the word that is the closest-matching dictionary word in the geometrical sense used by the keyboard algorithm, which happens to be "polite." The issue is that "oooorr" doesn't look enough like "polite" for our brains to close the gap between the two. They don't look like they go together. We don't accept **oooorr → polite** in the same way we accept autocorrections like **rhe → the** or **firdt → first**. The goal for autocorrection was to give you the word you meant, given what you did, not unconditionally conform your typing to the dictionary through the use of some clever calculation. As I developed the keyboard code, I found that it was sometimes better to leave the typed letters alone, and not substitute with an autocorrection, on the assumption that typists really did mean what they typed. After a certain point, unexpected autocorrections made the software seem confusing rather than helpful. Where was this point? I could find out only by asking people, and then, based on their feedback, picking a heuristic cut-off point for how much intervention I should allow the pattern skew algorithm to make and when I should have it back off. In this case, experience showed I should leave **oooorr** alone.

Other times we chained algorithms and heuristics together. The output from a heuristic often became the input to an algorithm whose output, in turn, became the input to the next heuristic. For example, swiping to the left to see the next image in the Photos app started with using your finger movement to make a judgment call for whether the swipe should go to the next photo or stay on the current one (a heuristic), which fed into animation code to move the photo display to a specific geometric position to center the next photo (an algorithm) starting from a certain speed, given how fast you swiped (another algorithm), and eased the photo to a gentle stop using a carefully designed animation timing (a heuristic).

This is what working at the intersection is all about. These examples should clarify why we always made so many demos. The photo-swiping example, in particular, should explain why you can't "engineer" a product in one phase and then slap on "look and feel" in another. It was often difficult to decide where an algorithm should end and a heuristic should take over. It usually took us many design and programming iterations to evaluate all the relevant options. The best solutions were an accumulation of small decisions carefully weighed against each other as we sought to tame the complexity of so many compounding and overlapping factors. The work could be like trying to fit together a jigsaw puzzle when we weren't sure what the final picture was supposed to look like, and the pieces kept changing shape. No single A/B test was possible. As software evolved through generation after generation, we could rarely see the full implications of any one choice in the moment of any one demo. We felt we had to live on the software over time to know for sure, to experience how the software fit into our lives, to see how what we were making measured up against our original vision. Our goal was to orchestrate a progression of algorithms and heuristics to create great products that would put smiles on people's faces and would function well without fuss. Design is, after all, how it works.

This is a slow road. As Steve said during the keynote introduction for the iPhone, he had been looking forward to the announcement for two and a half years.

* * *

With a product like the iPhone, the intersections are many, and some are of a different sort.

In the keynote presentation at Macworld when Steve first announced the iPhone, there was the intersection of my keyboard with the world. When Steve got to the exact point in the iPhone presentation where he would make the first public demo of the keyboard to people outside Apple, my feelings of pride and hope were displaced by fear and dread. Then in his description to the audience, Steve called my keyboard "phenomenal," and he successfully typed a text message. Whew! To be honest, Steve appended a stray return character on the end of his text, which he didn't intend, but no big deal. Nothing disastrous happened, and I felt a double dose of relief. The demo went fine. That was cool.

There was the intersection of me with Steve. Immediately after the iPhone introduction keynote, Richard Williamson and I walked to the front of hall, up to the stage, to gather with the rest of the Purple software development team. As we got close, we walked right past Steve. Steve looked over to us, and he recognized Richard immediately and thanked him. This was my first time meeting him; while he knew my work, he didn't know who I was. In the aftermath of the biggest Apple keynote ever, I walked up to The Man himself, and he looked right past me. That was disappointing.

There was the intersection of the iPhone with skeptics. It didn't take long after the Macworld keynote announcement for people to start proclaiming their doubts about the product, and perhaps none has become as famous as the derisive commentary from Steve Ballmer, then the CEO of Microsoft, whose first reaction to hearing about the iPhone was: "500 dollars? Fully subsidized? With a plan? I said that is the most expensive phone in the world, and it doesn't appeal to business customers because it doesn't have a keyboard, which makes it not a very good email machine."[9]

Time has proved Ballmer laughably wrong. Even so, in the immediate aftermath of the iPhone announcement, it was nice to get a sideways shout-out from yet another Steve. That was funny.

Turning closer to the point of this chapter, there's the intersection between the iPhone and our effort to create it, which brings me back to one of the basic questions I'm asking in this book. Why do some products, like the iPhone, turn out as well as they do? I'm now ready to offer my complete answer. It comes in three parts.

The first part is the demo-making creative selection process. Adding it to the concept of working at the intersection, I can enhance my description of how we created variations as we developed a product.

When we got an idea, we cobbled together a first cut on the algorithms and heuristics we would need to illustrate it. Then we pulled together the supporting resources—code, graphics, animations, sounds, icons, and more—to produce a demo. After we showed the demo and shared some feedback with each other, we made decisions about changes that might be an improvement. Many times this came down to tuning some heuristic, or modifying how an algorithm and heuristic combined. Whatever it was, the concrete and specific modifications we chose to make led to the actions items that justified making the next demo. Repeat, then repeat again. Doing this over and over again set our projects on the slow path to accumulating positive change. This is how we started with an idea and finished with software for a product.

The second part of my answer goes back to the introduction, where I first mentioned the seven essential elements of the Apple development approach. By now I hope you can see how essential they were and how they provided us with the raw material for creative selection. Here's the full list of the seven essential elements again, and this time, I've supplemented them with specific examples drawn from my stories:

1. Inspiration, which means thinking big ideas and imagining about what might be possible, as when Imran saw how smooth finger tracking would be the key to people connecting to iPhone experiences through touch

2. Collaboration, which means working together well with other people and seeking to combine your complementary strengths, as when Darin and Trey helped me make the insertion point move correctly in WebKit word processing

3. Craft, which means applying skill to achieve high-quality results and always striving to do better, as when the Safari team made the web browser faster and faster by running the Page Load Test, trying to understand what this test program told us about our software, and using these findings to optimizing our code

4. Diligence, which means doing the necessary grunt work and never resorting to shortcuts or half measures, as when we persisted through the tedium of fixing cross-references to get Safari to build in the lead-up to the Black Slab Encounter

5. Decisiveness, which means making tough choices and refusing to delay or procrastinate, as when Steve Jobs made me pick the better keyboard layout for the iPad on the spot while he waited rather than just offering the two different designs Bas and I developed

6. Taste, which means developing a refined sense of judgment and finding the balance that produces a pleasing and integrated whole, as when we made the choice to offer a QWERTY keyboard layout for the iPhone

7. Empathy, which means trying to see the world from other people's perspectives and creating work that fits into their lives and adapts to their needs, as when Scott Herz made a game to find the best size for touch targets so it was comfortable to tap the iPhone display and accommodated people with varying levels of dexterity

There are many more examples. It was inspiring when Richard made his initial browser demo to show the potential of the Konqueror browser code, and pulling off this demo in a couple days demonstrated his expert-level craft. When Greg Christie said, "Aww . . . come on, Ken!" to urge me to put one letter on each key for the QWERTY keyboard, it was one of the most decisive moments in my career. Continued diligence was necessary to build the autocorrection dictionary for the iPhone, adding all the entries and adjusting all the usage frequency values to create a lexicon of many tens of thousands of words. The tuning decisions for countless heuristics were made with impeccable taste by designers like Bas and Imran and could be seen in every gesture and interaction on the original iPhone. Empathy informed the design of the slide-to-unlock control to make it intuitive even for children. Scott Forstall gave me a chance to join the Purple project even after I botched the opportunity to manage one of his software teams—a collaborative leap of faith in me—because he thought I had something to contribute, and I just needed the right role.

There's something important I want to mention about these examples, because you might be thinking it yourself. Some of the instances I cite are small, seemingly insignificant. How much empathy did Scott Herz feel when he made his tap-target game? How much decisiveness did it take for Greg Christie to declare that I should go back to single letters per key for the QWERTY keyboard?

Such questions miss the point: We tried to be tasteful and collaborative and diligent and mindful of craft and the rest in *all the things we did, all the time.* Everything counts. No detail is too small.

This brings me to the third part of my answer. After creative selection and the seven essential elements, we needed one more intersection to make great work: a combination of people and commitment. Creative selection and the seven essential elements were our most important product development ingredients, but it took committed people to breathe life into these concepts and transform them into a culture. The culture we created is inseparable from the products we created. In my experience, this manner of culture formation works best when the groups and teams remain small, when the interpersonal interactions are habitual and rich rather than occasional and fleeting. The teams for the projects I've described in this book were small indeed. Ten people edited code on the Safari project before we made the initial beta announcement of the software, and twenty-five people are listed as inventors on the '949 Patent for the iPhone. Although these two numbers measure different things, they get us in the right ballpark. These weren't software teams of hundreds or thousands. There was a pragmatic management philosophy at play here, which started from Steve on down. Our leaders wanted high-quality results, and they set the constraint that they wanted to interact directly with the people doing the work, creating the demos, and so on. That placed limits on numbers. This had a follow-on effect as well, in that keeping our development groups small fostered feelings of personal empowerment and a sense of team cohesion. These factors are significant, especially since they're often at the top of the list of dynamics that managers of too-big teams try to instill and promote. Efficient communication was yet one more oft-elusive characteristic our small teams organically engendered. The communication paths among our few team members became well traveled, and these tracks became like ruts in a road, easing the journey to our desired destinations. We always tried to reach those destinations as quickly as we could, with a minimum of dithering and delay.

This last point speaks to the first important lesson I learned about product development at Apple, the revelation that results could be achieved more quickly than I had previously thought. Richard's initial web browser demo demonstrated to me how to get moving on a project, how to marshal inspiration, craft, decisiveness, and taste, and how to kick off a progression of creative selection. From the moment Don and I saw Richard's crystal ball version of Konqueror, we were willing to invest ourselves in the Apple-style get-it-done product development culture. We weren't alone either. The other people who found their way to Cupertino around the same time I did got the chance to participate on some outstanding projects, and when we recognized the opportunity, we banded together through our work, and we just kept going.

So, here's my take on the Apple Way, our recipe for making software for products like Safari, WebKit, iPhone, and iPad, my explanation for how we made great products:

A small group of people built a work culture based on applying the seven essential elements through an ongoing process of creative selection.

Expanded out, it reads like this:

A small group of passionate, talented, imaginative, ingenious, ever-curious people built a work culture based on applying their inspiration and collaboration with diligence, craft, decisiveness, taste, and empathy and, through a lengthy progression of demo-feedback sessions, repeatedly tuned and optimized heuristics and algorithms, persisted through doubts and setbacks, selected the most promising bits of progress at every step, all with the goal of creating the best products possible.

In this chapter about intersections, this expanded explanation fits right in. It's also highly *execution dependent*, as they say in Hollywood, meaning that the quality of the result is mostly in the quality of the doing.[10] This shouldn't be surprising, given that it's a matter of people, their tools, and what they choose to do with them.

My expanded explanation also serves as a statement of our product development vision, and we treated this as a practical problem. We assembled our tools and we got to work, hoping we could create designs and write code that would turn our dreams for great products into a reality.

10

At This Point

June 29, 2007, was a special day, and I decided to play hooky. Instead of heading into the office in the early morning and running through my usual routine—get coffee, sit down at my desk, scan the news, read my email, check my bug list in Radar, start programming—I stayed at home and surfed the web. After an hour or so, I drove from my house in Sunnyvale to downtown Palo Alto, about ten miles away. As I waded through the stop-and-go traffic in the morning rush on University Avenue, Palo Alto's main street, I craned my neck to look up the road. When I got closer, I saw a line was already snaking around the block. I parked my car and walked over to check out the crowd. I didn't have a specific goal for this trip, or even a clear idea for why I was going, except I wanted to be among people who were waiting for the Apple Store to open so they could buy their first iPhone.

A little more than six months after Steve's keynote presentation, the iPhone was *finally* going on sale. The long lead time between product announcement and its release was uncharacteristic for Apple, but there had been regulatory hurdles to clear before Apple could sell phones and getting an early start on the necessary public filings would have given away the secret about the product. So Steve decided to reveal the iPhone months ahead of the date that people would be able to purchase one. He did his best to use this time gap to the company's advantage, to make it seem like Apple was playing hard to get with its new smartphone, and at least among geeks and gizmo lovers, it succeeded. When the iPhone arrived in stores, many people couldn't wait to get one.

One of those people was Bill Atkinson. As I walked past the front of the Apple Store and turned left down Kipling Street in Palo Alto, and peered ahead to see the end of the line in the distance, I saw him. Bill Atkinson, the software virtuoso, graphics whiz, one of the visionary contributors to the original Macintosh, developer of revolutionary apps like MacPaint and HyperCard. Since Bill had left Apple long ago, he had to wait in line just like everyone else.

Except Bill was never just like everyone else. He was excitedly holding court for the small clutch of people around him who knew who he was. He was energetic, and he was waving his arms around a little. As I walked up to him, I noticed he was gesticulating toward something in his hand, a curious-looking, phone-shaped something. When I got close enough to see it more clearly, I still couldn't tell what it was, so I asked him.

Bill explained that he was so eager to get an iPhone that he couldn't merely wait, so he did what any unconventional genius would do. He went into his well-outfitted home workshop with a piece of fine-grained, light-colored wood, and he milled a model of the iPhone. Then he printed out a high-resolution clownfish photo, just like the one Steve used on stage during the keynote

announcement six months earlier, and he affixed the photo to his wooden model. In effect, Bill had made himself a toy iPhone. Just so he could hold it. I thought this was marvelous.

Bill and I had never met, but we knew many of the same people. I introduced myself after asking him about his wooden iPhone, and I told him that I had worked on the actual iPhone, though I'm not sure it registered. In any event, it was a thrill for me to see Bill Atkinson, one of the makers of the Mac, one of my heroes, waiting in line to buy his first iPhone.

Somehow, that felt like a mission accomplished, so I returned to my car and drove back to the Apple campus in Cupertino. When I badged into the Purple hallway, Scott Forstall was standing among a small group of programmers out in front of his office. This was unusual, but as I said, June 29, 2007, was a special day. When I walked over to him, I discovered he wasn't merely meeting and greeting people as they walked by. He was pouring champagne. Scott handed me a glass, and we toasted the release of the iPhone.

My clearest recollection of those first days after the first iPhone shipments was . . . relief. I was relieved that my keyboard worked well enough that it didn't sink the iPhone as handwriting recognition did the Newton.

Even so, that first iPhone had some glaring software gaps that seem remarkable now, and among them was a lack of cut, copy, and paste. It's hard to believe that the iPhone was out in the world for nearly two full years without a basic feature that had shipped with the first Mac in 1984. That's how technology development goes. The evolution of a new software system doesn't necessarily follow the same course as previous ones.

As we made the first couple annual revisions to our software, Steve and Scott were committed to keeping our development teams small and focused, to maintain the culture we had used to develop the iPhone in the first place. Although the software team did start to grow during these years, we were still just a few dozen designers and programmers, and we kept working as fast as we could to make the iPhone into a full-featured platform.

By the time we started on what would become iOS 4 (Apple changed the name of the iPhone software to iOS in recognition of the operating system's status in the company and its growing stature in the technology world), I got my promotion to Principal Engineer of iPhone Software (which shows Steve decided on the name change somewhat later in that yearly development cycle), and I started working on the iPad keyboard demo with Bas that we eventually showed to Steve.

After we shipped the iPad in 2010, Steve and Scott were interested in knowing whether the larger iPad screen size would make it easier to land several fingers on the display at once, enabling whole-hand gestures to control the experience of using multiple apps.

The original iPhone supported multitouch, and using pinch to zoom to scale a photo or a map was one of those intuitive gestures you see once and remember forever. Yet, as late as iOS 4, our software offered only two-finger gestures, even though the multitouch system could process as many as eleven simultaneous touches. You could, for example, mash the screen with all ten fingers at once and then reach down with your nose to tap the display. On the iPhone, obviously, there wasn't room to do that. The screen was too small. On the iPad, there might be enough display area for comfortable five-finger gestures, or so we thought.

Scott wanted to find out what these five-finger gestures would be like. He wanted an investigation into using the iPad's bigger screen to make better use of multitouch to make using multiple apps easier. We had made some software improvements for running multiple apps in iOS 4, and Scott wanted to expose this to users in a friendly way on the iPad. He pitched me on a goal for iOS 5: Add multitouch multitasking gestures for iPad. I signed up to do the work.

In a few weeks, I had a demo featuring early versions of three iPad multitasking gestures:

1. A *side-to-side swipe* to move between your most recently used apps without going back to the home screen
2. A *swipe up* to show a bar of icons of your most recently used apps
3. A *scrunch* to go back to the home screen from the current app

What exactly is a scrunch? I used the word to describe the gesture where you move your fingers on the screen in a grasping motion, as if the app you were using was a piece of paper and you were crumbling it up to throw it into a wastebasket. You know, a scrunch.

After a few weeks of polishing and more rounds of demos, we were feeling good about swiping, swooping, and scrunching. We were ready to show Steve.

In the fall of 2010, I walked through the door of Diplomacy, ready to demo iPad multitasking gestures. Steve, Scott, Greg, and Henri were there when I walked in. As usual, Steve was seated in an office chair. He looked exceedingly thin, but if he wasn't feeling well, I couldn't tell. Steve, Scott, Greg, and Henri sat on the mangy conference room couch facing him.

I figured that as soon as Scott was done with his introduction, I would begin my brief pitch before turning to the software. I was planning to say something like "Here are the multitasking gestures Scott was talking about. I have three . . ." But when Steve realized the topic was iPad multitasking gestures, he interrupted Scott, saying that he had been thinking about this feature, and he had come up with a way for going back to the home screen from an app. He then demonstrated his idea, waving his hand in front of his face like he was batting at a fly. After a swish or two, he made the gesture more specific, lowering his hand, bringing his palm parallel with the floor. Then he curled his fingers back toward himself, cupping his hand slightly, then he gave a quick outward flick of his wrist, like he trying to shoo an app away.

It was great to get an idea like this directly from Steve, and it was a clear depiction of a gesture that might be good. There was only one problem. I didn't have that demo. My return-to-home-screen gesture was the five-finger scrunch, not Steve's shoofly flick. I had no idea what I was supposed to do or say.

Scott came to my rescue. He explained to Steve that we had been developing these multitasking gestures for a while, that my demo was all ready to go, and he should take a look at what we had.

I woke up the iPad I was holding and took a step or two toward Steve's chair. I tipped the screen toward him so he could see, supporting the back of the display with my left forearm as I grasped the right-edge bezel of the device firmly in my fingers. I certainly didn't want the iPad to tumble out of my grip and fall into Steve's lap. After I read from Steve's body language that he could see what I was doing, I tapped a home screen icon to launch an app. Then I reached down toward the display with the open palm of my right hand, emphasizing the spread of my fingers. As I came close to touching the screen, I relaxed my hand slightly, letting my fingers take on a natural bend so that all my fingertips would meet the surface of the screen at the same time. When they did, I slowly scrunched, drawing all my fingers together. As I did this, the app shrank, zooming down incrementally in step with my gesture, until, when I let go, we were back at the home screen filled with icons.

Steve took the iPad from me, set his feet squarely on the floor in front of him, laid the iPad down in his lap, and tried launching and scrunching apps for himself. He made an overly large movement of his arm to draw his fingers away from the screen after scrunching. To be honest, it looked a little funny, but all I cared about was that every scrunch worked exactly as it should have.

He pronounced himself satisfied, and I was once again impressed by his ability to surrender his own idea when presented with a different one that worked. We moved on to the other two gestures, the swipe-up gesture that pushed up the current app to reveal an icon bar with recently used apps and the side-to-side swipe to move between your most recently used apps without going back to the home screen. I mentioned that the side-to-side gesture was something like his shooing-flick gesture, but Steve didn't react. He just continued looking intently at the screen and using the gestures.

Before long, Steve discovered one extra detail I'd put into the side-to-side gesture. As you swiped left or right, the full-screen representation of apps slid on and off the left and right edge of the screen. The display would show only portions of two apps at any one time—the one you were on and the one you were swiping to. As we were designing this lazy Susan for apps, we decided that if you launched an app by tapping its icon from the home screen, then swiping to the right wouldn't show another one. Since this side-to-side gesture was about getting quick access to your most recently used apps, and the app you just launched from the home screen was the "most recent" by definition, then there shouldn't be any more apps in that direction.

In my effort to communicate this, I had been inspired by the springy rebound you get when you reach the end of a scrolling list on iOS. I created an elastic animation for the side-to-side gesture, as if the most recently launched app was made of rubber if you tried to swipe to the right on it. The app stretched playfully in this situation, and when you let go, it snapped back into shape with a *bloop-bloop-bloop*. To me, this effect clearly conveyed that there were no more apps in that direction.

I thought the elastic animation was cool, but Scott hated it. He thought we would be taking liberties we shouldn't by stretching apps in ways their designers couldn't control. He could have insisted that I remove it, but I guess he sensed my enthusiasm.

Steve, in contrast, loved it. When he discovered this rubbery animation, he straightened himself a little in his chair, still balancing the demo iPad in his lap, and motioned at the screen with both hands outstretched, pointing definitively with all ten fingers toward the device in front of him. Without looking up, still staring at the display of the iPad, he declared his opinion on the elastic effect:

"This animation . . . this is Apple."

*　　*　　*

Several months later, in one of my regularly scheduled one-on-one meetings with Henri to discuss my continuing iPad work, I suggested to him that it might be a good idea to have another demo with Steve, to show him multitasking gestures again, now that the software was close to its final form. It would give him one more chance to give feedback before we shipped iOS 5.

Henri responded with a shake of his head and a matter-of-fact "At this point, I think we should go with the multitasking gestures as they are."

We finished our chat a few minutes later, and when I left Henri's office and made my way down the hall, I heard his words again in my mind.

"At this point . . ."

Then it hit me. Henri knew: Steve wasn't coming back.

About six weeks later, Steve resigned from his position as CEO of Apple. About six weeks after that, he was gone.[1]

Epilogue

For many years, working at Apple gave me financial stability, acceptance from a group of talented colleagues, and a worldwide reach for my software. Steve Jobs provided his single-minded focus on making great products, and his vision motivated me. Everything clicked.

In this book, I've spent much time discussing the lessons I learned during my Apple career. The biggest lesson I learned as I wrote this book is how a group of people and the culture they create are one and the same. After Steve died, the Apple software development culture started to change. As time passed and other coworkers came and went, the culture changed more. By my last day at Apple in 2017, few of the people I've mentioned in this book remained at the company, and more than anything, I missed collaborating with them as we had in the stories I've told. As I write, I still feel a strong bond to Apple, its products, and the people I worked with in more recent years, but it was time for me to move on.

A couple weeks before I resigned from the company, I worked on one final project, an exhibition for the Design Museum in London. Apple was putting together a display about the iPhone as part of an installation called *California: Designing Freedom*, which would feature many West Coast American influences, from the 1960s counterculture to Silicon Valley high tech. My contribution was to revive my original keyboard autocorrection code as an example of the multitouch operating system we invented ten years earlier. I retrieved the software from our source code archives, and I got it running on a modern version of iOS so some Apple designers could refer to it as they made a high-resolution animation of the keyboard for the museum show. It was a pleasure to look at that code—and spend a few hours with it—one last time before I departed.

Now that I've left Apple and devoted the time to write this book, my thoughts turn to the future.

As we look for new solutions to new problems, I suggest we turn to the tools I've described—the essential elements, creative selection, and a culture built around them. Naturally, it's possible to use any set of tools to do excellent or shoddy work, or to employ them to achieve worthy aims or trivial ones. We should choose wisely, because the iPhone demonstrates the societal impact a successful product can have, both good and bad.

I'd like to end with a note to readers at the beginning of their careers. You might be telling yourself that you want a career in product development. You may have plans to do great things in some other field. Either way, I have some advice: Get busy. Decide what it means to do great work, and then try to make it happen. Success is never assured, and the effort might not be easy, but if you love what you're doing, it won't seem so hard.

Acknowledgments

Thanks to Tim Bartlett at St. Martin's Press. You're reading this book because he put his faith in a first-time author. Thanks to Kim Scott for her steadfast support and for introducing me to Tim. Thanks to Alice Pfeifer at St. Martin's Press. She was endlessly helpful, patient, and answered all my questions. Thanks to Alan Bradshaw at St. Martin's Press for his assistance with copyediting and proofing. Thanks to Nick Ditmore and Bianca Bramham for helping to coordinate the full-page illustrations, and to Guy Shield for drawing them. Thanks to Andy Matuschak and Julie Whitney for reading early drafts and providing valuable feedback.

Thanks to my friends and colleagues at Apple. There are far too many of you to name, but you know who you are. I may be an introvert, but if I liked working with you, I said so. Thanks, folks. You gave me some of my happiest times.

Thanks to my wife, Jean. When it comes to happiest times, she's first and last.

Notes

2. The Crystal Ball

1. Free Software Foundation, *GNU Operating System.* [Online]. Accessed November 12, 2017. Various pages on this website provide the history, the philosophy, and licenses for the GNU Project. https://www.gnu.org

2. Steven Levy, *Insanely Great, the Life and Times of Macintosh, the Computer That Changed Everything* (New York: Penguin Books, 1994). The Mac has been an inspiration to me from the moment I first saw one in college in 1984, and if Steven hadn't written his book about how the people at Apple created it, you wouldn't be reading this book right now.

3. David Winton, *Code Rush: Full Film.* Vimeo. [Online]. PBS Home Video, Winton Dupont Films, April 25, 2000. Accessed November 12, 2017. One of my favorite scenes from the documentary showed Don walking across the Netscape campus in the fading light of early evening. A colleague, Tara Hernandez, was along for the the jaunt, and she was toting a hockey stick for reasons unexplained. They were off looking for a wayward software engineer who possessed an arcane bit of knowledge that might fix one of the few remaining bugs preventing Netscape from shipping the browser

code. When they found the engineer's cube, which was stacked high with empty Coca-Cola cans and other detritus, its owner was nowhere to be found. Where was this guy? Nobody knew. A cube neighbor of the not-found engineer, who had seen the engineer earlier in the day, heartily joined in the pronouncement of impending "Doom!" I thought it was a great show, the stuff of Silicon Valley legend. https://vimeo.com/8235099

4. Sam Williams, *Free as in Freedom: Richard Stallman's Crusade for Free Software* (Sebastopol, CA: O'Reilly & Associates, 2001). https://www.oreilly.com/openbook/freedom/index.html

5. Wikipedia contributors, "Gratis versus Libre," *Wikipedia, The Free Encyclopedia,* https://en.wikipedia.org/w/index.php?title=Gratis_versus_libre&oldid=840748752. Accessed May 14, 2018.

6. David Flanagan, *JavaScript: The Definitive Guide,* 3rd ed. (Sebastopol, CA: O'Reilly Media, 1998). O'Reilly & Associates books were ubiquitous in 1990s high tech. All the programmers I knew had these books and cherished them. While I haven't actually referred to my second edition of *Programming Perl* ("the camel book") in many years, I keep it by my desk out of sheer love and nostalgia.

7. "Steve Jobs Announces the Microsoft Deal—Macworld Boston" (1997). *YouTube: EverySteveJobsVideo.* [Online]. Accessed November 12, 2017. This keynote was presented at Macworld Boston on August 6, 1997, at the Bayside Expo & Executive Conference Center. Cue to 30m 20s to see Bill Gates. https://www.youtube.com/watch?v=almoJa_c_FA

8. James Daly, "101 Ways to Save Apple," *Wired,* June 1, 1997. The word "Pray" appeared on the cover of the magazine, but the article itself was titled "101 Ways to Save Apple." The advice was mostly wrong or dopey ("#1. Admit it. You're out of the hardware game. . . . 24. Pay cartoonist Scott Adams $10 million to have Dilbert fall in love with a Performa repairwoman. . . . #73. Rename the company Papaya"), but it does turn out that #50 did the trick: "Give Steve Jobs as much

authority as he wants in new product development." https://www
.wired.com/1997/06/apple-3/

9. "What Makes a 10x Programmer/Software Engineer?" *Quora*.
[Online]. Accessed November 12, 2017. https://www.quora.com
/What-makes-a-10x-programmer-software-engineer. "Are You a 10x
Programmer? Or Just a Jerk?" *The New Stack*. [Online]. Accessed
November 12, 2017. https://thenewstack.io/10x-programmer-just
-jerk/. Love the title. It communicates the doubt many in the indus-
try feel about 10x programmers.

10. Frederick P. Brooks Jr., *The Mythical Man-Month: Essays on Software
Engineering*, Anniversary Edition (Reading, MA: Addison-Wesley,
1995), p. 17.

3. The Black Slab

1. WebKit, "Timeline." [Online]. Accessed November 14, 2017. My
memory is good, but it's not good enough to remember exact line
counts to the level of accuracy I wanted for the text. I referred to
the open source WebKit repository for assistance on dates, chro-
nology, files, names, commit comments, and the like. https://trac
.webkit.org

2. Ryan Tate, "Apple Just Ended the Era of Paid Operating Systems,"
Wired. [Online]. Accessed October 22, 2013. https://www.wired
.com/2013/10/apple-ends-paid-oses/

3. Elmer Ellsworth Burns, *The Story of Great Inventions* (New York:
Harper & Brothers, 1910), pp. 121–124.

4. Steven Johnson, *Where Good Ideas Come From: The Natural History of
Innovation* (New York: Riverhead Books, 2010).

5. Paul Israel, *Edison: A Life of Invention* (New York: John Wiley &
Sons, 1998). Of particular interest is the text on pages 168, 188,
and 217.

6. James Newton, *Uncommon Friends: Life with Thomas Edison, Henry
Ford, Harvey Firestone, Alexis Carrel & Charles Lindbergh* (New York :

Harcourt, 1987), p. 24. Apparently, the author, James Newton, was on the scene when Edison made this statement about inspiration and perspiration. However, the quotation I cite is part of a lengthy back-and-forth with a reporter who was questioning Edison on the occasion of his birthday in 1929, and I doubt the author had a notebook to take down what Edison said. So, did Edison really talk about his working method exactly as we say that he did? I don't know, but posterity seems to be voting in the affirmative, and by using this quotation again myself, I realize I'm just adding another log onto the fire.

4. One Simple Rule

1. Donald E. Knuth, *The Art of Computer Programming* (Boston: Addison-Wesley, various years).

2. Donald Knuth, "Structured Programming with go to Statements," *ACM Computing Surveys* 6, no. 4 (1974): 261–301. I love how Knuth's famous statement on optimization comes in an article that references one of the other most famous statements in computer science, that from the age of "structured programming," the assertion made by E. W. Dijkstra in his article "Go To Statement Considered Harmful." That article can be found by consulting your friendly neighborhood search engine. I found it here: http://www.u.arizona.edu/~rubinson/copyright_violations/Go_To_Considered_Harmful.html

3. Cliff Edwards, "Commentary: Sorry, Steve: Here's Why Apple Stores Won't Work," *Bloomberg Business Week*, May 20, 2001. [Online]. Accessed November 13, 2017. https://www.bloomberg.com/news/articles/2001-05-20/commentary-sorry-steve-heres-why-apple-stores-wont-work

4. "Steve Jobs Introduces 12"–17" PowerBooks, iLife & Safari—Macworld SF" (2003). *YouTube: EverySteveJobsVideo*. [Online]. Accessed November 13, 2017. This keynote was presented at Macworld Expo

SF on January 7, 2003, at the Moscone Convention Center, San Francisco. Cue to 3m43s to hear Steve discuss Apple Store performance. https://www.youtube.com/watch?v=5iOWA2wEFPE

5. David Foster Wallace, *String Theory: On Tennis: Five Essays* (New York: Little, Brown, 2014). Is my passage about Vince Lombardi an attempt to channel Wallace? Yeah, maybe. The piece I'm thinking about the most is the one about Tracy Austin, published in this volume as "How Tracy Austin Broke My Heart." This piece appeared originally on August 30, 1992, in the *Philadelphia Enquirer.* The banal baseball quote I used is modeled closely on one Wallace used in his story.

6. John Eisenberg, *That First Season: How Vince Lombardi Took the Worst Team in the NFL and Set It on the Path to Glory* (Boston: Houghton Mifflin Harcourt, 2009), p. 76 (chapter 7).

7. Ibid.

8. *Lombardi.* HBO Sports, NFL Films, 2010. I couldn't obtain a full copy of this film. I found what appears to be an excerpt on You-Tube at https://www.youtube.com/watch?v=ILrJenuiYF0, and I could only deduce this clip came from the HBO production. I recognized Liev Schreiber's voice, and other sources confirm that he did indeed provide narration for the film. In addition, one other clip of Jerry Kramer shows him in the identical setting as a trailer for the film available on HBO's website. I am reasonably confident this citation is correct. I wish I could watch this HBO film in full. I reviewed a wealth of other Lombardi resources while researching this book, and these few clips from this truncated excerpt are among the best. The review of the film by Richard Sandomir that appeared in the *New York Times* on December 10, 2010, under the title "The Loud, and Memorable, Voice of Lombardi," cites NFL Films as "the main repository for film of Lombardi as a coach." Presumably, a more determined researcher than I could nail down these clips by approaching HBO or NFL Films. Off you go.

9. "Vince Lombardi Teaches the Power Sweep Part 1," *YouTube: Football Coaching*. [Online]. Accessed November 14, 2017. I wish I could obtain a full copy of Vince Lombardi's *The Science and Art of Football*. For the sake of nostaligia, a 16mm print would be ideal, to be viewed in a darkened room, with the light of the projector revealing chalk dust in the air. Sadly, I could only find excerpts of this film on YouTube. I found the film's introduction and portions describing the Power Sweep at https://www.youtube.com /watch?v=uv4CXySXxCk.

10. *Lombardi*, HBO Sports.

5. The Hardest Problem

1. Tracy Kidder, *The Soul of a New Machine* (New York: The Modern Library, 1997), pp. 82–83.

2. Wikipedia contributors, "White-Naped Xenopsaris," *Wikipedia, The Free Encyclopedia*, https://en.wikipedia.org/w/index.php?title=White -naped_xenopsaris&oldid=833595068. Accessed November 14, 2018. I edited the original HTML source to simplify it.

6. The Keyboard Derby

1. *NBC Nightly News with Brian Williams*. May 25, 2006. http://www .nbcnews.com/id/12974884/#.Ww3STy-ZP1I. This is such an apt summation of Steve's work philosophy that, after his death, when the company put up a remembrance to him in the atrium of Infinite Loop Building 4 on the Apple campus in Cupertino, these were the only words chosen for display.

2. Freddy Anzures and Imran Chaudhri, Graphical user interface for a display screen or portion thereof. U.S. Patent D604,305, filed June 23, 2007, and issued November 17, 2009. This is the design patent describing SpringBoard, the iPhone home screen icon launcher program. http://patft1.uspto.gov/netacgi/nph-Parser

?patentnumber=D604305; Bas Ording, List scrolling and document translation, scaling, and rotation on a touch-screen display. U.S. Patent 7,469,381, filed December 14, 2007, and issued December 23, 2008. This is the patent describing inertial scrolling. http:// patft1.uspto.gov/netacgi/nph-Parser?patentnumber=7469381; Matt Brian, "The Apple Patent Steve Jobs Fought Hard to Protect, and His Connection to Its Inventor," *The Next Web*, August 7, 2012. Accessed November 19, 2017. https://thenextweb.com /apple/2012/08/07/the-apple-patent-steve-jobs-fought-hard-to -protect-and-his-connection-with-its-inventor/

3. "Crackberry," *Urban Dictionary*. Accessed November 14, 2017. https://www.urbandictionary.com/define.php?term=Crackberry

4. Kenneth Kocienda et al., Keyboards for portable electronic devices. U.S. Patent 7,694,231, filed January 5, 2006, and issued April 6, 2010.

7. QWERTY

1. Mat Honan, "Remembering the Apple Newton's Prophetic Failure and Lasting Impact," *Wired*, August 5, 2013. https://www.wired .com/2013/08/remembering-the-apple-newtons-prophetic-failure -and-lasting-ideals/. Accessed November 14, 2017.

2. Wikipedia contributors, "International Talk Like a Pirate Day," *Wikipedia, The Free Encyclopedia,* https://en.wikipedia.org/w/index .php?title=International_Talk_Like_a_Pirate_Day&oldid=83104 8898. Accessed November 14, 2017.

3. Wikipedia contributors, "QWERTY," *Wikipedia, The Free Encyclopedia,* https://en.wikipedia.org/w/index.php?title=QWERTY&oldid =842348998. Accessed May 14, 2018.

4. Samantha, Today I Found Out, "The Origin of the Qwerty Keyboard," January 7, 2012. http://www.todayifoundout.com/index .php/2012/01/the-origin-of-the-qwerty-keyboard/. Accessed May 14, 2018.

5. Wikipedia contributors, "Critique of Judgment," *Wikipedia, The Free Encyclopedia,* https://en.wikipedia.org/w/index.php?title= Critique_of_Judgment&oldid=842429054. Accessed November 14, 2017; Immanuel Kant, *Kant's Critique of Judgement,* translated with Introduction and Notes by J. H. Bernard, 2nd ed. revised (London: Macmillan, 1914). Originally published 1892. http://oll.liberty fund.org/titles/1217. Accessed November 14, 2017.

6. Kant, *Kant's Critique of Judgement,* p. 62.

7. Quoted in Rob Walker, "The Guts of a New Machine," *The New York Times Magazine,* November 30, 2003. http://www.nytimes.com/2003 /11/30/magazine/the-guts-of-a-new-machine.html. Accessed November 14, 2017.

8. Richard P. Feynman, "Atoms in Motion," in Richard P. Feynman, Robert B. Leighton, and Matthew Sands, *The Feynman Lectures on Physics, Volume I.* http://www.feynmanlectures.caltech.edu/I_01 .html. Accessed November 14, 2017.

8. Convergence

1. Kenneth Kocienda et al., Method, Device, and Graphical User Interface Providing Word Recommendations for Text Input, U.S. Patent 8,232,973, filed June 30, 2008, and issued July 31, 2012. http:// patft1.uspto.gov/netacgi/nph-Parser?patentnumber=8232973.

2. Wikipedia contributors, "Bugzilla," *Wikipedia, The Free Encyclopedia,* https://en.wikipedia.org/w/index.php?title=Bugzilla&oldid=8413 48601. Accessed November 15, 2017.

3. stopdesign, creative outlet of Douglas Bowman, "Goodbye, Google," March 20, 2009. http://stopdesign.com/archive/2009/03 /20/goodbye-google.html. Accessed November 15, 2017.

4. Charles Darwin, *The Origin of Species* (New York: Collier & Son, 1909), pp. 45–46. I obtained a digital scan of this edition at https:// ia902205.us.archive.org/19/items/originofspecies00darwuoft /originofspecies00darwuoft.pdf.

5. Wikipedia contributors, "Seagull Manager," *Wikipedia, The Free Encyclopedia*. https://en.wikipedia.org/w/index.php?title=Seagull _manager&oldid=838557671. Accessed November 15, 2017. The original source for this notion appears to come from a book titled *Leadership and the One Minute Manager* by Ken Blanchard, published in 1985.

9. The Intersection

1. "Steve Jobs Introduces the Original iPhone at Macworld SF (2007)," *YouTube: EverySteveJobsVideo*. https://www.youtube.com/watch?v= -3gwlXddJuc. Accessed November 16, 2017. Cue to 21m45s to hear Steve begin his iPhone introduction. I believe the cue point isn't forty-one minutes because copyrighted content was shown on keynote day that can't be reproduced on YouTube.

2. "Steve Jobs Introduces Original iPad—Apple Special Event (2010)," *YouTube: EverySteveJobsVideo*. https://www.youtube.com/wa tch?v=_KN-5zmvjAo. Accessed November 16, 2017. This keynote was presented on January 27, 2010, at the Yerba Buena Center for the Arts in San Francisco. Cue to 1h30m to hear Steve talk about the intersection.

3. Robert X. Cringely, *Steve Jobs: The Lost Interview*. Furnace, Public Broadcasting Service (PBS) (as NerdTV), Oregon Public Broadcasting, John Gau Productions, 2012. Cue to 57m to hear Steve talk about proportionally spaced fonts on the Mac. http://www .magpictures.com/stevejobsthelostinterview/.

4. "Star Wars Blasters Sound Effect. How They Did It," *YouTube: ted-merr*. https://www.youtube.com/watch?v=fl0wIdGxfbQ. Accessed November 16, 2017; "The Story Behind the Creation of the Lasergun Sound in Star Wars." Filmsound.org. http://filmsound.org /starwars/lasergunstory.htm. Accessed November 16, 2017. "Sound Design of Star Wars." Filmsound.org. http://www.filmsound.org /starwars/.

5. Wikipedia contributors, "Ben Shneiderman," *Wikipedia, The Free Encyclopedia,* https://en.wikipedia.org/w/index.php?title=Ben_Shneiderman&oldid=838578865. Accessed November 16, 2018. Wikipedia contributors, "Direct Manipulation Interface," *Wikipedia, The Free Encyclopedia,* https://en.wikipedia.org/w/index.php?title=Direct_manipulation_interface&oldid=831492190. Accessed November 16, 2017.

6. Wikipedia contributors, "The Magical Number Seven, Plus or Minus Two," *Wikipedia, The Free Encyclopedia,* https://en.wikipedia.org/w/index.php?title=The_Magical_Number_Seven,_Plus_or_Minus_Two&oldid=841444468. Accessed November 16, 2017. George A. Miller, "The Magical Number Seven, Plus or Minus Two: Some Limits on Our Capacity for Processing Information," *Classics in the History of Psychology.* http://psychclassics.yorku.ca/Miller/. Accessed November 16, 2017. The article reproduced on this website was first published in *Psychological Review* 63 (1956): 81–97.

7. Steven P. Jobs et al., Touch screen device, method, and graphical user interface for determining commands by applying heuristics. U.S. Patent 7,479,949, filed April 11, 2008, and issued January 20, 2009. http://patft1.uspto.gov/netacgi/nph-Parser?patentnumber=7479949.

8. Ibid. The text I cite is in column 75, starting on line 39.

9. "Ballmer Laughs at iPhone," *YouTube: smugmacgeek.* https://www.youtube.com/watch?v=eywi0h_Y5_U. Accessed November 16, 2017.

10. The first time I heard the term "execution dependent" was when screenwriter Philippa Boyens used it to describe her effort to write the lines for Samwise Gamgee near the end of *The Two Towers. The Lord of the Rings: The Two Towers, The Appendices, Part Three, The Journey Continues . . . , From Book to Script: Finding the Story.* New Line Productions, Inc., 2002. "What does 'execution dependent' mean?" johnaugust.com. https://johnaugust.com/2009/what-does-execution-dependent-mean. Accessed November 16, 2017.

10. At This Point

1. Apple Newsroom, "Steve Jobs Resigns as CEO of Apple," August 24, 2011. https://www.apple.com/newsroom/2011/08/24Steve-Jobs-Resigns-as-CEO-of-Apple/. Accessed November 16, 2017. Apple Newsroom, "Letter from Steve Jobs," August 24, 2011. https://www.apple.com/newsroom/2011/08/24Letter-from-Steve-Jobs/. Accessed November 16, 2017. Apple Newsroom, "Apple Media Advisory," October 5, 2011. Accessed November 16, 2017.

Index